THE
MAYAN
OUROBOROS

THE
MAYAN
OUROBOROS

The Cosmic Cycles Come Full Circle
The True Positive Mayan Prophecy Is Revealed

DRUNVALO MELCHIZEDEK

WEISER BOOKS
San Francisco, CA / Newburyport, MA

First published in 2012 by Red Wheel/Weiser, LLC
Red Wheel/Weiser, LLC
With offices at:
665 Third Street, Suite 400
San Francisco, CA 94107

ISBN: 978-1-57863-533-7

Cover design by Adrian Morgan
Interior design by Happenstance Type-O-Rama

Printed in the United States of America

CONTENTS

INTRODUCTION

This book is a continuation of my last book, *The Serpent of Light*, and of the guidance our native ancestors are sharing with us. These ancestors are the living indigenous people who are still on Earth, and who, I believe, hold the keys to our future.

In my discussion with the Itza Mayan Council of Elders in the Yucatan, Mexico, in early 2011, it became clear that they believe that in the last minutes before the end of these cycles, on December 21, 2012, the Maya will be completely transparent to the world. They will not hide the secrets they have kept for thousands of years, but openly allow the world to know what they know, for they are aware for certain that you *are* them. And what happens to you happens to the Maya.

The Maya believe that they have a responsibility to the world to provide the guidance necessary for humanity to make a change to perceive the One Reality in a new way from one's heart. In other words, they wish to help leave this old world and enter a new world, which they believe is absolutely necessary at this time in history.

I will be just as open when it comes to revealing Mayan information. My intention is to assist all my relatives as they ascend—and we are all related.

When the White Snake bites its tail—the ouroboros—and is perfectly aligned with the cycles of the Earth, the Sun, and the center of the Galaxy, which are also biting their tails as the cycles come full circle, anything is possible. Will humanity respond and dream a new dream? Whatever happens will be in Divine Order, and as the events unfold, we will all soon witness the results of thousands of years of preparation by our ancestors.

This native information may contain the hope of the world, as the Ancient Ones are here now and ready to share with you an initiation into an ancient way of interpreting our everyday lives beyond what we have been told by society, religion, government, and our families.

We are in the moment of rapid change, and most of you can feel it. From my heart to yours, prepare for your world to open in unexpected ways.

In La'Kesh

Awakening
to
the Mayan Way of Perceiving

Life is always completing itself, by itself,

through itself.

There is no other!

OUROBOROS

**Only one spirit moves through All Life
everywhere
And everything is alive.**

SACRED GEOMETRY

PROVES

This One Universe of stars and planets was created
through the shape and proportions of a simple
sphere, and can equally be seen in a circle.

As you understand this, you understand the
importance of cycles.

Time is circular.

Space is circular.

Dimensions are circular. Size is circular.

Even all light waves become circular eventually.

So when a cycle of 25,625 years

comes to an end and a new beginning emerges,

perhaps we should see and know the sacredness in
the moment of our everyday lives.

Remember who YOU are in the dance of cycles,

and

you immediately win the Game of Life.

What's your prize?

Oneness reveals Itself

all around you

and

within you.

Polarity disappears.

Death is mastered.

Immortality becomes reality.

And YOU come full circle when you realize that

what is all around you, Nature,

Is also within you.

Do you know you are filled with stars!

YOU

are the connection between the outside

and

the inside

And truly,

the First _is_ the Last

and

The Last _is_ the First

Ω

In La'Kesh

Mayan for:

"You are another me, and I am another you."

The Mayan Ouroboros

DECEMBER 21, 2012

11:11 PM (Chitzen Itza, Mexico)

At that moment,

the Earth, the Sun,
and
the Center of our Galaxy
are in a straight line,
and it will not happen again

for 25,625 years.

Spiritually know:

At that moment, the Heart of the Earth, the Heart of the Sun, and the Heart of Our Galaxy as living beings are Intimately Connected.

Birth is inevitable.

December 22, 2012

12/22/2012

2222

A New Cycle Begins

The Window
Of
Global
Change

Is
Opening…

Part I

BREAKING SILENCE

Chapter One

SEDONA, 2007

The Mayan civilization is hidden, complicated, and difficult for the outer world to penetrate. There are many Mayan councils that have emerged in the last two decades, and they do not all agree with each other, much like it is around the world in other indigenous tribes, and for that matter, the way it is in the world in general.

The Guatemala Mayan Council of Elders was established in 2000. The president of this council is a man named Valerio Canche Yah. He mostly remains invisible, yet his power is very strong. Even though the legal documents say that a presidential term is three years, he has been in power since the council's inception.

Another member of this council is Don Alejandro Cirilo Perez, who has become the ambassador to the world for the Mayan people. He is a thirteenth-generation Mayan shaman and priest and is deeply respected by his people. He was a Mayan bright light to the world, speaking around the world including the United Nations attempting to help his people, but also trying to help the whole world. He also became the first indigenous Mayan to become an ambassador for the government of Guatemala.

There is another Mayan, Don Pedro Pablo Chuc Pech, who is also a member of the Guatemalan Mayan Council of Elders. I met him in Paris as we both spoke on stage to an audience of about 1,100 people. From the moment I met him, I realized that he was a great man, and my heart felt him as a brother. Don Pedro Pablo was given the title of the head of the Itza Mayan Council of Elders in the Mexican Yucatan, but he is such a humble man that he gives no importance to it. This was a council that was created mostly to interface with the industrial world. The Itza Maya are the largest tribe in all of Mayaland, which includes not only Mexico, but also Belize, Guatemala, Honduras, El Salvador, and other regions.

There is another Mayan, Hunbatz Men, whose full name is Hunbatz Mena, and is a member of the Itza Mayan Council of Elders. Hunbatz now mostly resides at the Lol Be Mayan Compound near the Mayan temple Chitzen Itza, where the modern Maya are attempting to remember their lost knowledge. Knowledge that was purposefully destroyed by the Spanish Conquistadors and the Catholic Church.

In March of 2003, Hunbatz Men invited me, and a world group that I formed, to give ceremony in the Yucatan. I will speak about this later. While these extensive ceremonies were being performed, the Mayan leaders above formed another council that may someday be of assistance to the world. It is called the Council of Elders of America, which brought together around three hundred indigenous elders who lead the tribes all over the Americas, not just Maya, but open to all tribes.

Though these indigenous tribes of the Americas may seem to be simple people who live deep in jungles and high on mountain-tops, they hold within their hearts information, knowledge and memories that will, at the right moment, become invaluable and necessary to the entire world. In your lifetime, you will understand.

We often forget that the Ancient World still lives within our society, and to this day is continuing to vibrate with the heart of Mother Earth, the heart of Father Sun, and the heart of the Universe to keep our fragile world in balance.

I believe that without the Maya and other global tribes that are part of the Maya, we would live in a world of utter chaos far beyond what we now are experiencing. Through the Maya you are about to witness a revelation of consciousness that will, according to the Mayan Prophecy, culminate in the birth of a new Earth and a new humanity.

To be certain, the Mayan Prophecy is a prophecy of great hope and beauty that begins on December 22, 2012, but the Maya are also realistic, and acknowledge that the old cycle and the old way of life will end on December 21, 2012. The window of time that centers on these dates will be explained in this book.

We must remember our past if we are to understand where we are headed in the future, for everything in the Universe moves in cycles, and the memory, knowledge, information, and wisdom that we need to ascend into higher consciousness is held in the DNA of our ancestors. We cannot push them aside and blindly forge ahead into the future, or the result will be catastrophic. We need them, and our living ancestors need us.

We have a singular chance to reconnect with our ancestors who are still alive on Earth in forms like the Maya and other native global peoples. We are doing this at the last minute of time before the Great Shift, but if we do so with our hearts open, we will find our way into the New World and all will be well.

The Serpent of Light Continues

We begin with a story that the Maya gave to me to give to you. It moves like a river, turning and changing direction, but always heading to the ocean, which for us is ascension. These stories will begin to narrow the gap between our understanding of the Ancient and the Modern World. They will shift our comprehension of how the Modern World interprets the Sun, the Earth, and our incredible Universe. If you can view what I am saying with your heart and not your mind, you will understand.

I will translate into the language of the Modern World what the Mayan people themselves are saying to me. Still, we are all different and understand differently. The human language is not perfect, but my intention is to reach your heart where I feel you will understand intuitively.

Guatemala, 2007

The Mayan Calendar is the most accurate calendar ever discovered on Earth. Humans are amazed at how an Ancient tribal people could be more precise than the Modern World and all of its technologies. Even today, the Maya are outperforming NASA and the world's scientific community when it comes to the cycles of time. Now humanity is looking to the Maya to understand this date of December 21, 2012 that is emphasized in the Mayan Calendar, and the Maya have responded.

In July of 2007, Don Alejandro Cerilo Perez and his wife Elizabeth came to Sedona, Arizona, where I live, to speak publicly about the Mayan Prophecy. The next day they met with me. They spoke with me about some of the Mayan prophecies and asked for assistance with these prophecies.

The first thing Don Alejandro told the public was that nothing we have read, heard, or seen about the Mayan culture and the Mayan Calendar was approved or written by any of the Mayan councils, and therefore was not spoken by the Mayan people. Everything we have learned about the Mayans has come from the universities, governments, religions, and archaeologists, lay people like Jose Arguëlles, and even some who are Mayan, but working on their own.

According to Don Alejandro, speaking to an audience of about 300 people, the Mayan Council of Elders of Guatemala, or any Mayan Council has not said one word to the world in 527 years (from 2007). That's a very long silence.

The Maya, in 2007, began to break their silence. You can see why this should be of great importance to the world. The truth about the Maya can only be spoken by the Maya themselves. A truth made up by outsiders who are simply guessing or who are living a consciousness that has almost nothing to do with the Maya cannot be valid.

The Maya wish to inform you that the world that you know, that you live within, is not what you think it is. We modern people think that the world is solid and real, and that nothing can change it except external events. We believe it is fixed and will go on for eternity with or without our presence. The Maya wish to inform you that this is not true.

The world is images that are created by consciousness and can be changed by consciousness through ceremony—especially consciousness that is connected directly into the human heart.

You are about to enter into a way of being that is only understood by the Ancient World; the Modern World has almost no idea of what we are about to discuss, and generally, it doesn't even know that it exists. And yet, this way of being is exactly what you, the Modern World, need at this moment in history, but you probably don't know it. Humanity is very much in the situation of a butterfly moments before it comes out of its cocoon. Everything it knew is about to change, and a completely new world is about to emerge.

Drunvalo

So why is a white man speaking about the Maya? In order to answer that question, I will have to tell you a little bit about my life. I'll keep it as brief as possible.

Like many people on Earth, when I was in my twenties, I wondered why I was here on Earth, and what life is all about. What is this planet and its brilliant Sun? What is really transpiring in our everyday lives? I had so many questions.

I became so intrigued with these ideas that I went to college and studied physics and mathematics—but not because I wanted to become a physicist or find quality employment. I thought that the physicists and the mathematicians must know what these stars and planets are, and studied for years and years until I finally came to the conclusion that scientists don't know any more about the Universe than I do. They are lost, and they too are searching.

I then switched from the left brain to the right brain and began to study art, art history, and painting. I spent two years studying 20,000 years of art history, from caveman to modern times, and slowly I began to get an inkling, through the female side of the brain, of what life was about. But the truth was still extremely elusive.

After I graduated from college, I decided to begin to study meditation. I had often heard that the answers to life were within, and it made sense. My first attempt at meditation was with the Hindus. Through them I was led to study mantras, the effects of sound on consciousness. The effects were so powerful that I found myself becoming serious about this method of understanding life.

One day while I was deep in meditation, an unexpected phenomenon startled me. I didn't ask for it to happen—it just happened. Two spheres of light, roughly sixteen inches in diameter, entered the room together floating in space and moved quickly up to me on both sides of my body about a meter away. They were brilliant lights. One was a beautiful ultraviolet color; the other one was a very bright green. I had no idea what they were, but for some reason I felt no fear, as though this was a normal event.

And then inside my head, telepathically, I heard these words: "We are not separate from you. We are you on another level of existence." I didn't know what they meant, but it made me curious about existence on a far more focused and fevered level. These two spheres of light began to lead me, and after over forty years, they are still in my heart and in my life.

Through my interactions with these two spheres of light, I was led to over seventy spiritual teachers around the world and studied many forms of meditation. At the same time, relevant to our discussion today, the two spheres of light also guided me into the indigenous world to begin the understanding of their ancient ways.

These two spheres of light soon informed me that they were "angels." They said that angels were formless beings, but took form in order to give human beings something to connect with. And they said that long ago they used the form of a human being with wings, but in truth, it is not their natural form. I had never had contact with an angel before, but their essence felt so warm and comfortable that I trusted them, and in all of these years, I still trust them.

Early in my relationship with the "angels," they led me to a tribe in New Mexico called the Taos. I spent fourteen years on or near the Taos Pueblo with the Taos. One of my mentors at the pueblo was a man named Tellus Goodmorning. He was in his nineties when I first met him, and he's now passed to the next world. He was the head of the Peyote Church for the United States, and he asked me to be his student. (Strangely enough, he never allowed me to take peyote. He said I didn't need it.)

Slowly, other members of the Taos Pueblo began to show me their ancient ways. One was named Juan Concha, the last chief of the Taos Pueblo who was given the title of the "kasiki," or the spiritual leader, by the tribe.

But I watched the inner work of these Native Americans unfold in my life, and I couldn't deny it. After fourteen years with the Taos, I had an indigenous training that changed my life. I was prepared to go out into the world to work with other tribes, which the Taos Pueblo said was my purpose in this lifetime.

The spheres of light then led me to what are called the Anasazi. They were the Ancient Ones who lived before the Hopi, the Sioux, the Lakota, the Cheyenne, and most of the other tribes we are familiar with. Through the Anasazi, I began to understand and know the sacredness of ceremony. Because of them, I was led to the Maya.

In 1985 I was directed by the spheres of light (through a man known as Thoth, the ancient Egyptian scribe) to go into the Yucatan, Mexico to study and do ceremony. Thoth is also someone who the Maya have had a long history with as he was the King of Atlantis while the Maya were living there. We will speak more about this later.

Thoth led me to do ceremony in sacred Mayan temples with names like Uxmal, Labna, Kaba, Chichen Itza, Tulum, Kahunlich, Palenque, and even into Guatemala to Tikal. It was an initiation for me, and the Itza Maya watched as I began to work on this level.

A few years later, I met Hunbatz Men, a Mayan priest and shaman who is connected with the Itza Mayan Council of Elders living in the Yucatan. He began to teach me the Mayan way of perceiving the world, which had different qualities than those of the tribes I was used to in the United States. In the late 1990s, Hunbatz asked me to perform ceremony with him, and for many years we were in ceremony together at various temples in the Yucatan.

Then for years I was asked to speak on their council, which I did to continue my relationship with them and to understand further their ancient ways. In the last couple of years the Itza Mayan Council of Elders has asked to be one of their council members.

In March 2003, Hunbatz Men asked me to come to Mexico, where we began to do deeper ceremony with tribes from all over Central and South America. My understanding of the true meaning of ceremony changed as I began to go deeper and deeper into the Ancient World and closer to the Source of Life. It wasn't until recently, in 2007, that I actually felt that I understood what ceremony means to the Ancient World. But the past ceremonies were necessary for me to reach this point where I could go beyond my white man education.

Evolving Consciousness

We know that human consciousness is evolving. Science has recorded this evolution over long periods of time. But in recent times, modern man has begun to accelerate its evolution in a way that most of us have not realized. Many of you are aware that the feeling of time is speeding up, but so is human evolution.

In the late eighties, the *Encyclopedia Britannica*'s editors released a major discovery: if you took all the knowledge that humanity had acquired since the beginning of our civilization, which began with the Sumerians about 6,000 years ago, and continued to 1900 AD, that same amount of information would double in the fifty years from 1900 through 1950.

During that fifty-year period, we learned as many bits of information, thinking in terms of computers, as we did in the previous 6,000 years! Nothing like this had ever happened in all of known history before.

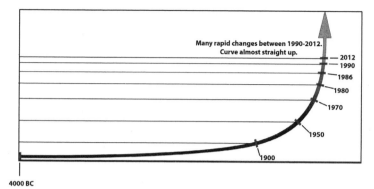

Many rapid changes between 1990-2012.
Curve almost straight up.

2012
1990
1986
1980
1970
1950
1900

4000 BC

The curve of knowledge from 4000 BC–2012

Then they discovered that from 1950 to about 1970 (these are approximate dates), humanity learned as much as we did in 6,000 years again, in only twenty years. But it continued, from 1970 to about 1980, and we again learned as much as we learned in the first 6,000 years. And it kept speeding up to about 1986 or so, when it doubled again. It is still continuing to accelerate.

There was a time in the eighties when the information that was being collected from space and Earth was flooding in so fast that NASA couldn't even download it into their computers. They were eight or nine years behind the entering of the data they had collected. They had to wait until the hardware and the software caught up to humanity's ability to learn.

Today, we are on a straight-up curve. We are learning as much as we learned in 6,000 years every few weeks now. This seems impossible, but it's true.

The Sanskrit Vedas, written about 6,000 years ago, speak about this time we now live in. They talk about how we learn about electricity and magnetism; they mention that "we learn to fly in the sky with metal boxes,"—that's actually a quote. And then on a single day, according to the Vedas, we give it all up. Much like a child as he grows older and lets go of his teddy bear and reaches for a higher vision, humanity will do exactly that—let it all go. That may be harder to believe than ascension itself, but life is full of surprises.

From the Mayan point of view, high technology is not a sign of an advanced civilization—it's an indication of a civilization that is about to be advanced. What good is technology to a people when they discover that the human body and human consciousness are capable of doing everything that technology is now capable of doing and far, far more? Would we not let go of external technology if we discovered that inner technology was vastly superior? The Maya believe that this realization is going to change us forever.

When we look back at the ancient cultures, it becomes clear that we humans are now very different than we were, say, 2,000 years ago. That's pretty obvious: not just our modern techno-toys, but different in how we perceive the very reality around us, what we think the reality is, and who we think we are within this reality. The Mayas say that we are about to go through a change of great magnitude, a change in consciousness. We are becoming something brand new, a new species with a new way of perceiving reality. That's really what this date of December 21, 2012 is about: a change in human consciousness that we call ascension. We are going to talk about many other subjects, but this is always the primary direction we are headed. Human consciousness is approaching a narrow point in time when human evolution speeds up tremendously and makes a jump into a new level of consciousness. We become something greater than what is now called human.

With this understanding, we will return to explain what the Maya have to say about what we are about to become. We will be cognizant of this understanding when we speak about human consciousness changing. First it is mandatory to remember what ceremony is, for it is within ceremony that our ability to ascend will be rediscovered.

Ceremony

In the Ancient World, ceremony meant far more than what we in the Modern World can even begin to grasp. Ceremony is direct communication and a living bond with Great Spirit, Mother Earth, Father Sky, and All Life Everywhere. The Ancients believed that before any harmonious change in the human world could take place on Earth, a ceremony had to be performed. Ceremony is what links our hearts and the heart of the Earth and the heart of the Sun and the heart of the Universe and everything and everyone that exists.

When people from the Ancient World entered into ceremony, they entered into a sacred world of infinite possibilities. The Maya have predicted that as we approach the years between 2012 and 2015, humanity will enter into chaos on a very deep level. But you will have no reason for fear. It is not the end; it is the beginning. Is it the end of the cycle of time and the end of the world? Or is it the beginning of a new cycle of great beauty and hope? This is what we have to discover.

If we focus on the end of the cycle as we look at the world around us, we see that everything in modern times, right now, is beginning to degenerate and break apart on vast and primal levels, exactly as the Maya predicted long ago.

Take, for example, global warming and the environment rapidly approaching a probable Ice Age (first it warms up) that would eliminate most life on Earth. The world's financial system is on the verge of total collapse, which we are struggling with all around the world. Diseases such as HIV/AIDS, H5 and H5N1 viruses, and other diseases threaten world pandemics. There are over forty wars occurring at this moment—in addition to Afghanistan and the Arab Spring, there are many other wars going on globally that we ignore. Even more painful, approximately four billion people are living on less than two dollars a day, and 25,000 children starve each day. A human population reaching seven billion people continues to expand to the point of destroying all life on Earth simply by existing.

I could go on, but your heart knows what I'm speaking about. The times we live in are precarious, to say the least. According to the Maya, all of this chaos was predicted long ago. We are approaching the end of a very long cycle, and this chaos always happens when the cycle ends. It's part of the cycle of life and death. It's natural.

The Maya predict that this chaos we are now experiencing is just beginning. Something far more powerful than anything we are now experiencing or have ever experienced in our memory is about to appear on Earth.

It's time we all listened to what is coming and prepare inwardly. It is not a time to continue to live as though everything is normal, for it is not. But what replaces the normal reality is far, far greater.

But while the coming change will have plenty of negative consequences, there is a positive aspect that the Maya and I want you to be aware of. Yes, there probably will be Earth changes, but there is something else far more important, extremely beautiful, and positive, that no one is discussing and most of science is unaware of. This is a message of great hope.

Whether this end of the Mayan Long Count cycle is a human disaster or a blessing for all of humanity will depend on humankind itself, as was explained to me not only by the Maya but by many other tribes. At a time like this, when a page in history is being turned and civilization is in crisis, everything depends upon how humanity assimilates all of its known experience, knowledge, and wisdom into a body of awareness that leads humanity into the future.

If this future experience is sustainable, then we survive; if it isn't, we go the way of the dinosaurs and become extinct. It is up to us. We have the power to change our future now. In fact, the here and now is the only place and time possible to make this change.

When we speak of this new consciousness, there is a paramount understanding, or secret, about how this higher consciousness actually manifests. I could put this into a sentence, but the sentence isn't understood by most people when I say it. I'm going to say it anyway, and then come back and explain it more.

This leap in consciousness can only be acquired when the awareness of the Ancient World is combined with the awareness of the Modern World.

Simply put, we live in both the Ancient World and the Modern World simultaneously, but with great difficulty. These two worlds need to understand each other and absorb each other's knowledge and wisdom, or neither will be able to move upwards into a higher consciousness. This requires cooperation.

The Ancient World is ready to move now. Most of the tribes of the entire world are ready for change. But the Modern World has still not understood the need for its ancestors—the Ancient World. Why are our ancestors important to our survival, and furthermore, why is our survival important to our ancestors?

The Maya of Eternal Time

In this Modern World, most of us live in a synthetic reality. By synthetic I mean separate from nature in our houses, our cars, and even our shoes. Our technology shields us from the outside world and the perils of nature, but it also shields us from an essential electrical connection to Mother Earth that all indigenous people understand. (I suggest that you educate yourself about a new science that has developed called Earthing at *www.earthing.com*.)

Because of our pride in technological achievements, we can't imagine why an indigenous person, with his or her feet in the dirt and barely able to feed him- or herself, could possibly have any kind of effect on this Modern World.

Let me explain why the Maya and other tribes are so important to humanity for our very existence. If you allow this understanding to give birth within yourself, you can go on into the hidden world of the Mayan people, where they will begin to reveal their way of life and wisdom to you.

Sacred Geometry

Looking into nature and the Universe, we see that the human body and all known life forms are governed by a mathematical series of numbers called the Fibonacci Sequence (more on that later). Our human body actually contains these patterns of numbers in billions of places, for every cell contains them, and proportional relationships of many parts of our own bodies correspond to them.

Sacred Geometry is the underlying blueprint of the Universe. It gives order to what would otherwise be total chaos. The arrangement of every single materialized object in existence, regardless of size, is brought into order through the geometrical patterns that we call Sacred Geometry. Planets orbit around the Suns with precision according to Sacred Geometry.

The Ancient World completely understood this, as evidenced by the vast Sacred Geometry embedded within each of the Pyramids, but the Modern World has forgotten this basic knowledge, and for the last 500 years has been in the dark. Now that NASA has remembered this ancient knowledge and is combining it with modern knowledge, a clearer picture of the Universe is emerging. Without this ancient knowledge, we could never know the truth of reality.

The Golden Mean

In my understanding, the Golden Mean, also called the phi ratio, is paramount beyond all other ratios and proportions in the Universe. You can take any straight line, no matter how long it is, and cut it in a particular place to create the Golden Mean. The smaller part of this line will equal one, and the longer part will be approximately 1.6180339, which is an irrational number that continues on for infinity. It's a proportion you can see not only in planets, stars, and moons, but also in any life form on Earth, including your own body.

If you look at the joints and bones in your hand and divide the length of the bone that includes your fingernail into the length of the next one, the phi ratio appears: 1.6180339. If you then take the length of that bone and divide it into the length of the next bone in your finger, the phi ratio appears again. You will find the Golden Mean ratio in all of your bones.

I feel certain that the Golden Mean is the most important proportion/ratio of all the other possibilities of mathematics that exist. Even the actual size of the planets and their moons is not an accident, but perfectly match Sacred Geometry.

But for life, you, me and All Life Everywhere, we don't know how to create the Golden Mean ratio. In fact, I don't believe the Golden Mean actually exists naturally anywhere in the Universe. It's only this idea, this ideal proportion, but in nature, the Golden Mean is only approximated. It doesn't actually exist in nature anywhere. Life doesn't know how to use numbers that never ever end. But didn't I say that the Golden Mean is found throughout your body? Am I contradicting myself? Let me explain.

Life figured out this awesome proportion from the very beginning of creation, but a man named Fibonacci rediscovered it only a few hundred years ago. The Fibonacci Series goes 0, 1, 1, 2, 3, 5, 8, 13, 21, 34, 55, 89, 144, and so on. It simply is a series where you add the first number to the next number in the series to arrive at the new third number. So if you start with 5 and add it to 8, the next number is 13.

But if you divide these numbers into themselves with the Golden Mean ratio of 1.6180339 (approximately) as your goal, you begin to understand. You divide 1 into 1, you get 1, and this number is under this Golden Mean proportion. If you divide 1 into 2, you get 2, which is over the number, but it's closer to the actual number. Then when you divide 2 into 3, you get 1.5, which is closer to this number, but it's under. When you divide 3 into 5, you get 1.666667, which is over but closer again. And if you watch this, as you continue to divide the smaller into the larger number you keep getting closer to the Golden Mean ratio of 1.6180339. By the time you divide 34 into 55 and get 1.6176, you are getting very close.

A nautilus shell

Here is a nautilus shell that's been cut in half so you can see inside. Each chamber is being created from the Fibonacci Series. You see these chambers at first are kind of unevenly spaced and very strange, because these chambers in the beginning of the nautilus shell are not close to the Golden Mean. The first chamber is the number 1, and then it continues, 1, then 2, then 3, then 5, etc. The first chambers are not very close to the Golden Mean, and your eye can see how off it is. As they get higher in the Fibonacci Series, they get closer and closer and closer to this perfect Golden Mean. You can see it taking place right before your eyes in this nautilus shell as the chambers get more and more perfect.

This is what life does. In order to get around the fact that it can't use these complex irrational numbers, Life has found a way to use single digit whole numbers only, like 1 and 2 and 3. And life uses these numbers not only in your bodies, but in every single thing alive on Earth including things that we do not consider alive, such as crystals.

Remember, what we are talking about here is why the Ancient World and the Modern World need each other in order to survive the Mayan Prophecy. I will explain this using the image of a sneezewort plant. It's a strange-looking plant, but it actually grows according to the Fibonacci Sequence; you can see the Fibonacci Sequence unfold before your eyes. As it comes out of the ground, it first grows 1 leaf, then 1 more; then it grows 2 leaves, then 3, then 5, then 8 leaves, and then 13 flowers.

The question to you is: How does this plant know, after it has grown 5 leaves, how many leaves it will grow next? Eight leaves is the answer, but why not 10 or 12 or some other number? How does it know that?

Sneezewort plant

The Fibonacci Sequence of the sneezewort plant

It knows what to grow because the plant looks back at its past, which is 3, and it knows that when it adds its past to its present, 5, the future is located at 8. It knows exactly that the number is 8.

This is the situation that humanity is in right now. The Modern World is like 5 right now, and it doesn't know where it's going because it's completely disconnected from its past. But when and if it reconnects with the Ancient World, and when it adds the Ancient World to the Modern World, it will know exactly where it's supposed to go. We can't know where our consciousness is going to expand to without reconnecting to the Ancient World. It's essential. It's not an option. We must. The Ancient World is completely prepared for us. They are ready. They know they need us. We just don't know we need them. This is the problem. But it is one I believe you will solve.

Chapter Two

WHY DECEMBER 21, 2012?

The Mayan Calendar is the most accurate calendar on Earth. This extreme accuracy has astonished scientists around the world, and partly because of its accuracy, hundreds of millions of people are looking to the Mayan Elders to explain the significance of December 21, 2012.

We know this date is important, but most of us don't know what it truly means. To help bring it to a brighter light, we will have to speak about other cycles of time. We will explain these concepts in the proper order, as they are all interrelated.

Modern science confirms the key to the Mayan Prophecies related to the magnetic pole shift of the Earth, and if the Maya are right, what is about to happen is nothing short of world-changing. Is there anyone out there who cares?

The Maya hope so. As academics have studied the Mayan Calendar, they have mostly come to the conclusion that 2012 is the year of the great doomsday for humanity. But when fully open to view from the living Mayan perspective, it would be more accurate to call it the birth of a new humanity, or to be clearer, the birth of a new consciousness. But this part of the prophecy has been completely hidden to most of the world. So far!

The National Mayan Council of Elders

Just so you understand the source of what I am about to say, I will quickly explain the National Mayan Council of Elders of Guatemala and who they are. There are 440 tribes living mostly in Mexico, Belize, Honduras, El Salvador, and Guatemala, and each of these tribes has one elected elder. These 440 elders make up the Mayan Council of Elders, centered in Guatemala. The council elects one member to preside over the whole council and the Mayan Nation. In 2007, this was Don Alejandro Cirilo Perez, who probably knows more about the Mayan people and their culture than anyone on Earth.

To be clear, there are other councils, such as the Itza Mayan Council of Elders centered in the Yucatan, Mexico—which I have been part of for many years. Then there are smaller councils located in Belize and Honduras and other places. These are mostly regional and meet the needs of the more remote Maya.

Here's what Don Alejandro told me about the Mayan Prophecy of 2012. First of all, he said there is a window of time around this date, December 21, 2012, that the Maya call the *End of Time*. It is about seven to eight years in duration. This window began, as I understand it, on October 24, 2007, but we have not been told the exact date it will end. If the window is eight years long, the window will close around November 2015. But for certain, at this moment, we are all living in this window of the *End of Time*.

Don Alejandro also said that the likelihood that the Mayan Prophecy will begin on December 21, 2012, as most people in the world believe, is extremely unlikely. He simply said it will begin somewhere in the window of the *End of Time*, which means any minute from now to perhaps as late as November or December 2015.

To further grasp this situation, we need to understand what the date of December 21, 2012 actually is, and to do that we must begin by talking about the Precession of the Equinox.

The Precession of the Equinox

On the Mayan Sun Calendar, there are wheels within wheels all synchronizing together. All of these wheels or cycles appear to be moving at different speeds, just like an old watch. One of these wheels is the Precession of the Equinox, which comes back around every 25,625 years.

Hidden within the Precession of the Equinox you will find five perfect Mayan Long Count cycles of approximately 5,125 years. If you multiply 5,125 by 5, you get 25,625 years, which is the exact length of the Precession of the Equinoxes, plus or minus a tiny bit.

There are four times when these 5,125-year Mayan Long Count cycles don't align with the Precession whatsoever, but once every 25,625 years, those two cycles come into perfect alignment, and that's what will happen on December 21 and December 22, 2012.

Let's take a closer look at time so we can see how this bigger picture emerges, and see what this Precession of Equinox is within this larger picture.

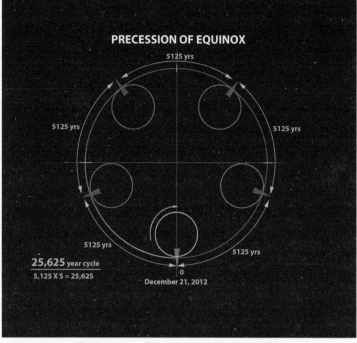

The five Long Count cycles within the POE

Time is an elusive human concept. Someone says, "What time is it?" We look at our watch and say, "Well, it's four thirty-two," but most of us forget on a daily basis that this "time" is connected to the rotation of the Earth, a real thing, not a virtual reality digital mind thing.

We look at the Sunrise or Sunset and we think, "The Sun is moving," but really it is only the rotation of the Earth that is causing this illusion—the same movement that creates our everyday time. The Earth spins one full revolution, and we experience a single day; this single cycle is divided into twenty-four segments, which we call hours. Of course we know this. Everyone knows a day is one revolution of the Earth.

The second best-known Earth cycle or wheel is the journey that the Earth makes around the Sun. One cycle around the Sun is one year, or 365.25 days. Some scientists say it's 365.44 days. And so it is clear that we count time by the movement of the Earth relative to the Sun, but there are other movements and cycles within and connected to the Earth that are less understood by most people on Earth, though they can still have an effect on our everyday lives just as the hours we record on our watches.

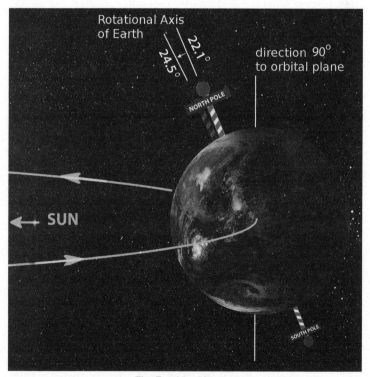

The Earth's obliquity

For example, the angle at which the Earth's axis is tilted to the Sun has an enormous effect on every human on Earth. At this moment the angle, called the Earth's obliquity, is about 23.5 degrees. This angle to the Sun creates our seasons—our spring, summer, fall, and winter.

The actual tilt of the Earth changes from 22.1 degrees to 24.5 degrees over an approximately 42,000-year period. Now this is a really long period, and you wouldn't think it would have anything to do with everyday life, but even with this long cycle, astronomers, for example, must take into account the changing tilt of the Earth's axis on a daily basis as they explore the Universe with their computerized telescopes. If they don't, instead of looking at what they think they are supposed to be looking at, they'll end up looking at something else!

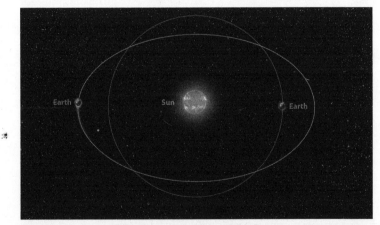

Earth's journey around the Sun

Even our journey around the Sun is not as simple as it seems. The shape of the Earth's orbit, called its eccentricity, is constantly changing. Our Earth moves from a near-perfect circle around the Sun to an ellipse over time, caused mostly by the gravitational influence of Jupiter and Saturn. This cycle, too, is changing over a very long period of time, about 100,000 years, but interestingly enough, this does not change the length of a year as it moves from a circle to an ellipse and back again.

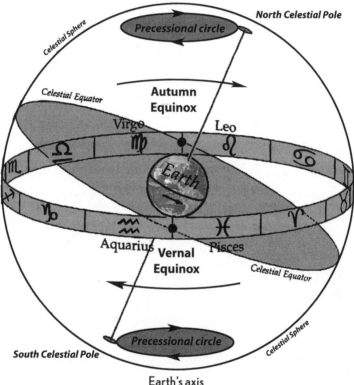

Earth's axis

And then there is the Precession of the Equinox, which is caused by a wobble in the axis of the Earth. The causes of this wobble are primarily the Sun and the moon, though other bodies do affect it. For years, our college textbooks said that the length of the Precession of the Equinox was

25,920 years. But in the year 2000, with new data from our spaceships, science recalculated the length of this cycle to be 25,771.5 years—the time it takes for the axis of the Earth to make one complete rotation.

As you see in the drawing, the Earth's axis is moving in an ellipse that wobbles. For it to complete one cycle, one wobble, scientists now say it takes 25,771.25 years. This estimate of the Precession of the Equinox's length of one cycle is perhaps getting more and more accurate, but it seems that the ancient Maya have a more perfect calendar (based upon the movements of the cosmic bodies) than modern science has.

The Precession of the Equinox is also always changing because of something called the Milankovitch cycles. The Milankovitch cycles are the summation of all the Earth's cycles and all other processes that affect the Earth's cycles.

Scientific study of the Milankovitch cycles has mostly focused on their effects on the Earth's climate. To study the Earth's climate, one has to know the Milankovitch cycles as well as the Sun's solar cycles.

Then of course there is also the orbit of the moon, which causes the tidal evolution and like a clock determines the high and low tides of our oceans, which affects the Milankovitch cycles as well.

These moon cycles also affect human emotions, and millions of biological cycles of all life on Earth, such as the female menstruation patterns. *These cycles are the key to everything that we are talking about and to all of the prophecies of the Mayan people.*

Now we can see that there are many cycles within the movements of the Earth. The Precession of the Equinox is simply one of them with influence on all the other cycles.

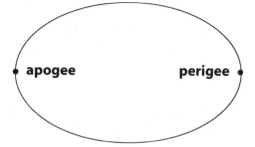

The elliptical pattern, and the apogee and the perigree

There are two points on the ellipse that are the most distant points from its center. These are called the apogee and the perigee, and they will become more and more important as we progress.

Further, during this cycle of 25,771.5 years, the Earth's axis also moves through all twelve signs of the Zodiac, and the axis of the Earth actually points to two different zodiacal signs at the same time as it moves. But from our way of thinking, on December 21, 2012, the axis of the Earth will begin to point at the sign of Aquarius, and according to the Ancient World, we will begin to change our consciousness.

The Mayan Hunab-Ku

We have looked at some of the logical aspects of the movements of the Universe. But there is something else that the Maya know that we often overlook. It is not just the male logical movements of the cosmic bodies that create the changes we experience; in addition, the timing of events is influenced by something that is mostly outside of science. You might call it the female side of the Universe.

Around the turn of this century, scientists discovered that there is an axis to the entire Universe—not just our galaxy, but literally everything that exists. This axis controls cycles of time in ways that we are just beginning to understand. Science has also noticed that the speed of light changes when you aim light exactly parallel to the Axis of All. Slowly, we are beginning to know the differences that this axis influences.

Yes, our great science just discovered the Axis of All, but the Maya have known this from the beginning, and they call it the Hunab-Ku. It is the axis of the Universe, but it is also the pattern that all patterns derive from. You could call it the Cosmic Seed that everything came from.

But what is important for us to understand is that the timing of events in the Universe is not fixed upon the male logical moments in space and time. Look at a solar eclipse. The timing of this kind of event can be predicted to the second, but it's meaning for humanity and its manifestation many not happen concurrently. This meaning may happen shortly before or after the eclipse, depending on the "right" timing according to the female nature of the Universe. It is not logical, as it is based upon feeling. This means that there is always a window of time when cosmic events take place.

And this is true with the alignment of the Earth, the Sun, and the center of the Galaxy. This alignment will take place on December 21, 2012, but when will humanity feel the changes?

Now let's look at this date of October 24, 2007 that began the *End of Time* window around December 21, 2012. What was special about this date?

The Hopi Prophecy and the Comet Holmes

There is another indigenous tribe in the United States called the Hopi who are related to the Maya. The world's academics believe that this tribe came across the Bering Strait from Russia to Alaska, walked down the coast of Canada, and eventually migrated to where they are now in northern Arizona.

According to Grandfather Eric, a member of the Hopi Council and the historian for the tribe, the Hopi did not arrive in Arizona via Russia. Instead, they migrated from the opposite direction. They came up from Guatemala, and when they left from Guatemala, they were Maya, not Hopi. The Maya sent them north for reasons that have to do with the time we are now in. The fact that the Hopi were originally Maya was acknowledged before me by both tribes; I actually sat and listened to them as they told this whole history.

Grandfather Eric is the last living member of the Blue Bird clan, which records the tribe's history. In November of 2007, Grandfather Eric and I were riding in a bus in Guatemala, sitting beside each other and talking, and he asked me if I saw the blue sphere in the sky on October 24, 2007. I told him I didn't actually see it live, but I had followed it on the Internet.

Then I told him that my daughter, Mia, watched it as it expanded, getting larger by the hour. She called me after 1:00 AM on the 25th of October. She was high in the red mountains surrounding Sedona where the night sky is dark and open. Mia said the moon was full or almost full and that Comet Holmes seemed bigger to her than the moon. "What was that blue sphere, Daddy?" she asked. All I could say was, "Honey, I have no idea. I have never seen anything like this before in my life."

A few hours after this cosmic event began, the Internet began to light up around the name Comet Holmes.

I told Grandfather Eric about the photo on the Internet that compared the comet's expanded blue sphere to the size of the Sun, which showed the comet to be slightly larger.

I expected Grandfather to answer me with something about the size of this cosmic event, but he looked at me and said, "Could this be the blue star prophecy that was prophesized over 200 years ago by our tribe?" I smiled and said, "Come on, Eric, only the Hopi will know the answer to that question."

But here's what happened, according to recorded science. Just before October 24, 2007, a comet named Holmes moved into our solar system—a very small, fast-moving comet. No one thought too much of this cosmic event; it wasn't a big deal.

Then, on October 24, 2007, this comet exploded with incredible force and rapidly became a huge blue sphere in the sky, expanding and expanding until it became physically larger than the Sun. It is now recorded as the largest object ever observed in our solar system.

Here is the photograph of Comet Holmes in its expanded state. You can see that it's bigger than the Sun. And by this we don't just mean optically bigger, but physically bigger. On the left is Comet Holmes and on the right is our Sun.

As I understand it, when Grandfather Eric arrived back in Hopi land, the Hopi Council met to discuss whether this blue sphere was in fact the Blue Star that was prophesized over 200 years ago within their tribe. It is hard to tell if the

Hopi will ever speak publicly about this. I experience them as mysterious people who have a deep sacred purpose, and they only say what they have to.

Comet Holmes in its expanded state

Comet Holmes
Explosion

Sun

Photo of Comet Holmes—blue sphere and the Sun side by side

However, after speaking with the Maya, I believe that most Maya feel that the Blue Star did mark the beginning of the *End of Time* window. The beginning of the *End of Time* wasn't just a random event. It was one of the biggest events that ever occurred in our solar system that we know of, ever.

There is a second part of this Hopi Prophecy: the coming of a Red Star that will mark the end of the *End of Time*. The Maya and the Hopi have not discussed this with me, though I know this has been written about in a few books.

What astronomy is witnessing at this moment could be the Red Star the Hopi are watching for. One of the four stars that surround the Belt of Orion, Betelgeuse (commonly known as "Beetlejuice"), is imploding at this very moment, and scientists believe that if this star stops imploding and begins to explode, it will become a supernova. If this happens, we here on Earth will feel this explosion rather dramatically, and Betelgeuse will become a huge red star in the night sky. Scientists also believe that there is a very good chance that we here on Earth will feel this explosion rather dramatically since we are so close to this star. It is expected to occur at any minute.

The Mayan Prophecy and the Pole Shift of the Earth's Axis

When Don Alejandro was in Sedona, Arizona in July of 2007, he described a piece of the Mayan Prophecy, but what he gave was only a small part of a huge event. There is more to come concerning what happens beginning on or after December 22, 2012.

What Don Alejandro did say—and this is Mayan Prophecy—is that there will be a *physical pole shift* of the Earth's axis sometime within the *End of Time* window. This means that we will not know if the Mayan Prophecy has happened or not until the very end of 2015, regardless of what happens on December 21, 2012.

The suggestion that the Earth's physical axis may shift to a new location is a huge statement, of course, but it is nothing new. Edgar Cayce, the American Sleeping Prophet, gave this same prophecy in the 1930s. Cayce said that sometime after the winter of 1998, the axis of the Earth would shift to a new location. He even gave the exact position to which he predicted the axis would move, a very specific point inside of Russia, approximately sixteen degrees from where the physical pole is now. (Cayce gave about 12,000 predictions from the 1920s to 1970, and was only wrong once, about a small matter.) So many scientists have been intensely watching the possibility of a pole shift because Edgar Cayce predicted it.

A physical pole shift always begins with a magnetic pole shift, and science has noted that the magnetic field of the Earth began to weaken about 2,000 years ago. About 500 years ago there was a dramatic shift in the strength of the magnetic field as it became weaker and weaker. Then, about forty years ago, the Earth's geomagnetic field became so weak that the magnetic lines that had been more or less fixed for a vast time began to change and wander.

This resulted in the beaching of whales that use the guidance of these magnetic lines for migration, something we had never seen before. Some of the lines now entered into landmasses for the first time. No one had ever seen the magnetic lines change like that before. Later, birds began to appear in locations that were not part of their migration patterns. There have been numerous anomalies all over the

Earth with life forms not responding in their natural patterns because of the rapidly changing magnetic field.

In the 1990s, the aeronautical maps of the world used for landing modern airplanes at airports had to be changed worldwide because the old maps were simply no longer valid. Today the magnetic lines are again so unreliable that magnetic maps have to be checked every single time a plane takes off or lands to make sure that their guidance systems are functioning properly.

In 2003, a *NOVA* television special called "Magnetic Storm" gave a team of global geophysicists the airtime to talk about the possibility of a magnetic pole shift. These scientists felt that the Earth's magnetic poles would shift sometime in the imminent future, but they could not say exactly when. Their concern stemmed from what they were observing at the Antarctic—huge holes forming at the South Pole where the magnetic lines were coming out of the Earth for a distance and then bending back and returning into the Earth, making the Earth's geomagnetic field even weaker.

Here are a few quotes from some of the geophysicists who appeared in that television special. Peter Olson (Johns Hopkins University) said, "The Earth's magnetic field has been our protector (from solar storms) for millennia, and now, it appears, it's about to go away." John Shaw (University of Liverpool) remarked, "The Earth's magnet field is getting weaker rapidly." Jeremy Bloxham (Harvard University) said, "The question is not if that's going to happen [magnetic field going to zero], it's when that's going to happen."

The following image is the accepted depiction of the geomagnetic poles of the Earth by present-day science. The magnetic lines of the Earth come out of the Earth at the South Pole, and then move external to the Earth until they reach the North Pole where they move into the Earth again to eventually emerge out of the South Pole, and then continue back to the North Pole. And for you scientific types, yes, the physical North and South poles are reversed for the geomagnetic North and South poles, but we didn't want to confuse most people.

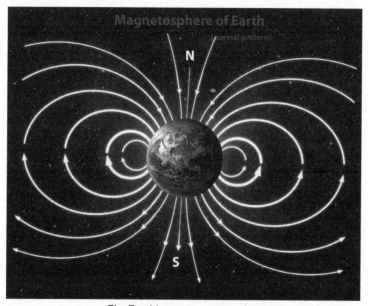

The Earth's geomagnetic poles

The Earth's geomagnetic field is getting even weaker faster now. Holes are forming at the Antarctic where the magnetic lines are leaving the holes, but then turning around and entering back into the hole that they came out of. If this continues, eventually all of the Earth's geomagnetic field will move back into the Earth and the magnetic field of the Earth will move to zero. Obviously, these scientists were very concerned, and you should be too when you understand what this could mean for you.-

The magnetic lines of the South Pole

In approximately 2009, scientists who study the Earth's magnetic fields, many of the same ones who spoke on *NOVA*, went onto the Internet to warn the world. They had eleven days before the government shut them down out of fear of public panic.

The scientists wrote that there are so many anomalies in the Earth's magnetic field that they believe that within twenty-five years, the geomagnetic field of the Earth could not only move to a new location, but could switch its polarity, meaning that the geomagnetic North Pole would become the South Pole and the opposite.

In 2011, these same scientists went back on the Internet with an even stronger warning. They said that the anomalies had become so great that they feared the possibility of a magnetic pole reversal any minute. The government shut them down after only five days.

What science knows is that a little less than 13,000 years ago, there was a physical pole shift. This pole shift coincided with the opposite end of the Precession of the Equinox.

Science also believes that Hudson Bay was the site of the physical North Pole before this axis shifted, and that approximately 25,625 years ago at exactly the very point we happen to be at this moment in the Precession of the Equinox, the Earth's physical poles shifted a second time.

If that is not shocking enough, science believes that when the Earth's physical axis shifts to a new location, it only takes twenty hours—less than one day. You wake up one morning, and in a single day, your world is completely transformed. The Maya believe it takes about thirty hours for the physical poles to shift, just for a reference.

When I met them in Guatemala in 2007, the Maya also agreed that there had been two times in the last 26,000 years when the Earth's physical poles had shifted. In their hearts and in other secret ways, these events have been recorded. The Maya remember what happened, and how people reacted to the rapid changes, which is why the Maya want to help you. To the Maya, you are one with them.

Now I need to discuss a new subject to bring light to what I have spoken about above. This will take a moment, and then I will return to the subject of the geomagnetic field of the Earth.

The Schumann Resonances and the Pole Shift Information

What is written above I believe is the truth, but something began to happen a few years ago that is very discouraging. It appears that some governments have decided that this information should not be told to the world. These governments may be trying to keep people calm, which is understandable. So I will tell you my story, and you can decide for yourself.

The Schumann Resonance (SR) is a fundamental standing wave of vibration that is contained from the surface of the Earth within a cavity that is created by the ionosphere above the Earth. These frequencies are generated by the summation of all lightning strikes hitting the Earth at a given moment. The Schumann Resonance has been stable for a very long time at a fundamental 7.86 Hz, so stable that the US Army even used it to calibrate their instruments.

In the early nineties I began to study this Earth energy, and I found that Gregg Braden was also studying it. Once he began to take it on, I was so busy that I simply waited to see what he found. We both noticed that the fundamental resonance seemed to be rising. Gregg began to gather data from two or three different universities in the US. Gregg found definitive hard evidence that the Schumann Resonance was rising with the written records from at least two US universities. These records showed that the Schumann Resonance had risen to 9.6 Hz.

By somewhere in the middle to late nineties, Gregg and I verified that Germany and Russia had both agreed that the Schumann Resonance was hovering around 9.6 Hz. But there was still a great deal of speculation as to what this meant for life on Earth. Realize that many people see this as the breath of the Earth.

Then Gregg began to write about the SR and how he believed that it would follow the Fibonacci Series and continue to move up in frequency until it reached about 13 Hz. Gregg also began to relate it to the rising of human consciousness to the next level. It was then that the US government began to make changes in the records. They obviously didn't want Gregg to talk about these things.

Suddenly, in one day, all the records at the universities across the US were altered, showing no change in the SR. They literally showed the SR had always been at 7.86 Hz. Both Gregg and I talked about this, but what can you do when something like this happens?

In my discussions with the Russian National Academy of Science of Moscow, they are showing that the Schumann Resonance at its fundamental level is approaching exactly what Gregg Braden predicted, just under 13 Hz.

It now appears that just as information about the Schumann Resonance at US universities was changed, so was information concerning past physical pole shifts. I had a hard time with the reasons why the government didn't want discussions around the SR, but I do understand why the government doesn't want information about the physical pole shift of the Earth to go public. If the shift proves true, the government would be the last to acknowledge it—after all, they have to maintain stability. Yet we need to know if we are to survive.

It's important to understand that it has been known for a long time that there have been hundreds of pole shifts of the Earth's axis extending over the last 400 million years.

It is a natural event and happens all the time. It is not this information that they are trying to hide, but only the last two pole shifts, which gives so much support to the possibility of a pole shift now.

The logic behind why the last two pole shifts support a pole shift now is because pole shifts usually come in swarms. You will see no pole shifts for a period of time, and then a pole shift happens. But it is seldom a lone pole shift. There are usually many in a row. And since we have had two in a row, it would be expected that there would be another at this exact moment in the cycles.

The Maya believe that we have had two pole shifts in the last 26,000 years and are due for one during this *End of Time* window. This was corroborated by scientists the last time I looked, but now it is not. Now scientists say that it has been almost 780,000 years since the last pole shift. Will our government go to any means to hide the truth? If you'd like to see for yourself, look for old records from before the year 1994, if you can find them.

Back to the Geomagnetic Field of the Earth

What scientists have also noticed is that directly before the Earth's physical pole shift, there is always a magnetic pole shift, followed by a period of a collapsed geomagnetic field. The magnetic field shuts down completely, and there are no North or South Poles for a period of time before the magnetic field begins again. From my understanding, this period of time is about two to four weeks long. But this remains only a theory for modern man, who has never been alive to witness the event, unlike the Ancient Maya.

Scientists have always wondered about this possibility of the Earth shifting its axis to a new location. Mathematically, it is almost impossible. The Earth is an enormous gyroscope with a mass so high that it would take such a tremendous energy to move it to a new axis location. There are very few scenarios to explain how this could happen—it would take the moon colliding with the Earth to move the axis of the Earth. And yet we know it is possible, because it has happened hundreds of times in the past. Axis shifting is definitely a natural phenomenon, but it has remained a mystery until recently.

Late last century, a scientist suggested a theory that has now been proven to be possible by at least two universities. It isn't something that one would just think up, as it requires deep knowledge of the Earth's interior. And now in 2012 this is the *only* theory that exists to really explain how the Earth can shift its axis on a continuing basis. This theory is the one that most scientists have now accepted as the most likely way the Earth shifts her axis.

The Earth has a crust, which is about five to thirty kilometers thick. Relatively, it is very much like the shell of an egg. Underneath the crust is the upper mantle, which is a ridge layer about 100 to 200 km thick. This upper mantle is a rock layer that sticks or holds the crust to the rest of the Earth.

However, what science has discovered through experiments at several universities is that the upper mantle is only ridge rock as long as the geomagnetic field exists. If the Earth's geomagnetic field were to stop and move to zero, after about two to three weeks, the upper mantle would turn to a liquid-like substance. It would become like oil.

When this upper mantle becomes liquid, it separates the crust from the upper mantle and allows the crust to move freely on the surface of this liquid-like substance. When that happens, the amount of energy required to move the surface or crust of the Earth to a new location has dropped to a very small fraction of what it would take to move the entire mass of the Earth. Even so, it still needs a huge amount of energy to move the crust of the Earth. Where is that energy coming from?

Scientists have recorded that the ice formation at the South Pole is off-center of the Earth's axis. It is a massive accumulation of ice about two miles high—So much ice that if it were to melt into the oceans, it would raise the surface of the entire world's oceans roughly 267 feet. If both the North and South Poles were to completely melt, it would raise the oceans about 297 feet, only thirty-two feet more. So you can see that most of the ice above water is in the Antarctic.

It has been theorized that if the Earth's crust were suddenly free to move, this off-kilter massive ice formation would move to the center of the axis and force the crust to move into a new position. We humans would experience this as a physical pole shift, and, relative to the equator, we would in fact be located in a new area of the Earth's surface.

In other words, this would not be a real pole shift, as almost all of the physical mass of the Earth would continue rotating around the same established pole, and the Earth's gyroscope would barely have been affected. But we humans would have moved to a new location relative to the heavens.

Amazingly, this is probably exactly what has happened so many times in the past, and probably what we are about to experience here on Earth in the near future, if Edgar Cayce and the Mayan Prophecy are correct.

Edgar Cayce predicted that the new pole of the Earth will be about sixteen degrees into Russia (Siberia, to be exact), and the mathematical scientists have calculated about seventeen degrees into Russia, into almost exactly the same place. This scientific prediction is completely based upon how far the ice mass at the South Pole would move the Earth's crust if it were free to move. We do not know if this is true or not, as nobody has ever seen this happen. Perhaps you will have a chance in your lifetime.

According to Don Alejandro, in the last pole shift, millions of people died simply because they didn't understand what was happening. If only they understood the situation, they could have easily transformed their experience into something of strength, grace, and beauty.

But Don Alejandro says that if they don't understand what is occurring and enter into fear, they can easily die. And so he wants to talk to you about this. He says that so many people died during this period because of fear, but that if you don't worry, simply stay still and just relax, everything returns back, your sight comes back, everything returns to normal. So this is another thing that the Mayan people want you to understand: during this change, don't go into fear. There is nothing to be afraid of.

Don Alejandro also speaks about thirty hours of darkness that happens at the moment when the poles shift. Some people out there, including myself, speak about three days of darkness. The Mayans say, "No, it's not three days, it's thirty hours." Everything goes black, and one cannot even see the stars at night. In other words, we go blind, and since our brain and sight are so physiologically connected to the magnetic field, that seems possible.

After the poles shift, of course your location on the surface of the Earth is probably completely different relative to the Equator than before the shift began. You are now probably living in a new and different environmental location on the Earth, and this must immediately be evaluated. You've got to figure out where you are or you could die just from extreme cold or extreme heat. This is another thing the Maya want you to know.

But understand that this is just the beginning of the Mayan Prophecy—the part that the world has named the "Doomsday" prophecy. There is something that is far more important. How do we understand how to *be* during a physical pole shift and directly afterwards? Here is the simple secret. Live what the Maya are suggesting below, and you will know immortality.

Chapter Three

THE HEART OF
THE MAYA

The depth of the heart of the Maya can be said in words, but it can only be lived and experienced to know the meaning and understanding. Words are from the brain, but what we need to remember has nothing to do with the brain, it has to do with the human heart.

I will use words, for they are all we have at this moment. I could say that within the heart is a sacred space where creation takes place, and that living within this sacred space changes one's relationship to all of nature and to the Universe.

The brain has an ego that sees itself as both separate from reality and as the most important part of reality. But within the human heart, one is not separate from the reality; rather, he or she becomes One with it. There is no separation, and all parts are equal. The Maya speak about this constantly, how no human being is greater than any other. We are all the same and of the same value.

As you can see, words may describe what we are talking about, but you cannot taste this other way without actually entering into the sacred space of the heart and feeling and becoming one with this ancient vibration. I am limited by words, so there is nothing I can do but choose my words carefully.

Guatemala

Perhaps the best way to show you the heart of the Mayan people is to begin with the story they gave to me to give to you. As you enter into the jungles of Guatemala, use your inner vision and senses. Remember your intimate connection with God. If you read this as a child, you have a better chance of remembering who you really are.

In June of 2007, I turned my manuscript for *The Serpent of Light* over to my publisher. The book includes many stories of the movement of the kundalini of the Earth and the sacred ceremonies of the Mayan people and other tribes. It describes how the interior energies of the Earth were altered.

As mentioned previously, in July of 2007, Don Alejandro visited Sedona and spoke publicly about the coming physical pole shift of the Earth. He discussed how the Spanish conquistadors had destroyed almost all of the Mayan artifacts and records, and how the Maya have subsequently lost most of their knowledge, prophecy, and wisdom. Don Alejandro spoke of secret documents that had been hidden from the conquistadors, and how the time had come to rebuild their ancient knowledge. He said that according to the Mayan Prophecy, the Maya had to begin to reconstruct their knowledge, their experience, their wisdom, and their memories—that this was the time that this had to be initiated and that during this time "the world would be watching."

The next day, Don Alejandro and I had a personal meeting. He told me that very soon, according to the Mayan Calendar, the world was going to enter into the *End of Time*, and that certain ceremonies had to take place in preparation. The exact times by which these ceremonies had to be completed were marked in the Mayan Calendar. This was still about three months before the blue sphere created by Comet Holmes appeared in the night sky.

Don Alejandro said that the Guatemala Mayan Council of Elders understood that "the world would be watching." He was referring to a group of people coming from all the continents and a vast number of countries around the globe who would represent the world. He asked me to find these people, exactly sixty of them, and gather them together in Guatemala City on a specific day in November of 2007.

From there, Don Alejandro and the Guatemala Mayan Council of Elders would take these representatives into the jungles of Guatemala to watch the Mayan Council begin to bring their knowledge together and perform ceremony with this world group.

Well, this was easy for me. It took sixty phone calls and it was done. The representatives came from twenty-three countries and five continents. In this invited group were Grandfather Eric from the Hopi Tribe and three elders from the Sierra Nevada Mountains in Colombia: a Kogi Mamos, an Arhuaco Mamos, and his brother, a normal Arhuaco. The Kogi and Arhuaco are significant because of the ancient past. Don Alejandro told me that the Maya were originally from Atlantis; so were the Kogi and the Arhuaco. I had known this for years, but it was pretty powerful to hear this from Don Alejandro.

Just to be clear, there are two other tribes living on the same mountain range with the Kogi and the Arhuaco—the Wiwa and the Kankuamo. They also came from Atlantis, but now they do not want to be part of the energy that has to go out and meet the world. Let's discuss Atlantis for a moment to see why these three tribes—the Hopi, the Kogi, and the Arhuaco—are so important at this time in history.

Atlantis

The symbol for Atlantis was in the shape of the City of Poseidon, the capital, and it was three rings—one ring inside of the other. The outer ring stood for the ordinary people who lived in Atlantis. The middle ring stood for the priesthood—who were called the Maya. Exactly the same name we call them today. The priests were the bridge between the people and the consciousness of the center ring, the Nakkals (sometimes spelled Naccals).

The Nakkals were the special ones who spoke directly from the Source of All Creation found within the heart of every person. There is a place within the physical heart of everyone that is the most sacred space in the Universe. This place is the source of all physical and nonphysical things in the Universe, including human bodies. It must be realized from within the heart for it to be known.

The Sacred Space of the Heart is a purely female center. She holds the image of the uterus, and the ultimate Source of All Creation. We think that only a baby can be born from the uterus, but when her uterus is connected to the Sacred Space of the Heart, all things are possible. Even objects like planets and stars can be created and come out of her.

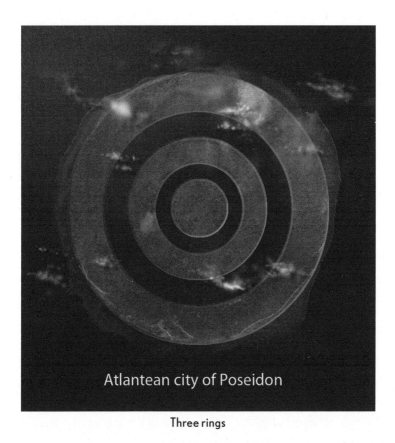

Atlantean city of Poseidon

Three rings

The Nakkals taught that All of Creation came from the union of opposites—male and female, macrocosm and microcosm. It is during the orgasm inside the female uterus when it is directly connected to her sacred dreaming heart that creation manifests.

The Nakkals were just like the Maya in every way, except they were living and breathing from their hearts and connected directly with the heart of Mother Earth, the heart of Father Sun, and the Heart of the Universe. In Atlantis they lived in special rooms within the pyramids in total darkness.

They glowed in the dark with bioluminosity, and floated a few inches off the ground. Their human bodies had broken the bonds with gravity, and in this state of consciousness they kept the world in balance and harmony.

All of this worked beautifully until humans in Atlantis misused major energy sources, directly altering the stability between the third and fourth dimensions of the Earth. But that ultimately led to a twenty-first-century miracle, not a disaster, as you will see.

It's clear now why the present-day Maya, linked by their DNA to the ancient past of Atlantis, are also linked by their DNA to other tribes who came from Atlantis. These primary tribes, and there may be others, are the Hopi of Arizona, the Kogi Mamos, the Arhuaco Mamos, the Wiwa Mamos, and the Kankuamo Mamos. All five of these tribes are linked directly with the Maya, and they all acknowledge it. The four Sierra Nevada Mountains tribes from Colombia are descendants of the Nakkals.

There is one more tribe: the Tibetans. They left Atlantis about 200 years before it sank into the ocean, and traveled to what is now Tibet. They also have the bloodline of the Nakkals, and they also will acknowledge this.

When Atlantis sank about 13,000 years ago because of the physical pole shift we just mentioned, the Maya jumped into their boats and rowed to the Yucatan, not far from the southwest area of Atlantis. The remaining Nakkals rowed their boats close to where Santa Marta, Colombia is now. All of these tribes remember what happened, not only at the end of Atlantis 13,000 years ago, but as far back as 26,000 years ago, and even much longer.

The 2007 ceremonies in Guatemala would be the first time since Atlantis sank that all of these tribes would be together to perform ceremony. According to Grandfather Eric, he would be the first Hopi to return to Guatemala since the tribe left Guatemala thousands of years ago to head north to the Four Corners area. This would be historic.

The 13,000-Year Guatemalan Ceremony

From all over the world, men and women gathered in Guatemala City to be part of a secret sacred ceremony for the awakening of the Earth. There were exactly sixty people in our group, as well as the small staff that had come together to help Mother Earth through her transition.

When we arrived at Lake Attila, one of the most sacred lakes of the Maya, our group was met by twenty-five members of the 440 elders. They had been elected to be the ones to begin the remembering of their knowledge.

There are other ways the Maya remember their ancient knowledge besides using their brains. Soon we will discuss the thirteen crystal-skull ceremony to reveal a completely different way of recalling ancient memory.

The world group sat down in a half-circle around the twenty-five Mayan elders as they began with the Mayan glyph for the number zero. They began to decipher this glyph as if they had never seen it before. After about an hour and a half, the Mayan elders had completed the number zero. Then they went to the glyph for the number one. We watched them as they went through zero, one, and two. We spent about a half a day witnessing this event, and then our part was over. The world watched as the Mayans began to recreate their knowledge. The prophecy was being fulfilled.

0   1   2

The Mayan glyphs of the numbers zero, one, and two

The Ceremony at Lake Attila

The next morning, the Mayan Council of Elders took us by boat to the far side of Lake Attila, to a sacred Mayan ceremonial location. We were there to hold an ancient Mayan fire ceremony.

Lake Attila and the volcano

The boat ride over was something that every person will probably remember for the rest of their life. A towering volcano perched on the very edge of the lake left me with an ominous feeling that it would explode at any moment. I mean, the mountain had black smoke pouring out of it. No wonder the Mayans had a fire ceremony there!

The beach on Lake Attila

We reached a remote beach, with the sound of the waves lapping endlessly and the deep blue sky forming the heavens above us. Don Alejandro shaped our diverse group into a circle, and in near silence, after an hour-long preparation with each stage of the fire ceremony, carefully created a beautiful geometrical arrangement of rocks, herbs, candles, and other sacred objects. Everything was ready for the fire to give life to the ceremony.

Typically indigenous people will not allow us to photograph, let alone videotape, these sacred acts. But that day the veil was lifted. The Elders actually let us record them making the geometrical images on the ground. They told us the meaning of each herb and candle as they placed them in the sacred bundle. According to Don Alejandro, this ceremony had not taken place for almost 13,000 years.

The Hopi, the Kogi Mamos, the Arhuaco Mamos, the members of the Guatemala Mayan Council of Elders, Don Alejandro, and our humble group from all over the world lowered our heads in prayer as the first flames began to reach the open sky.

Though we were from all over the world and from many different traditions and cultures, we all entered into our hearts and emerged in prayer with one voice and one heart. We prayed for Mother Earth and for her children, knowing that the Earth was about to enter into a very violent stage of evolution, much like childbirth. Each one of us prayed from our hearts for Mother Earth to help the world and all life on her.

This ceremony was three hours long, and about one hour into it, as I was watching the flames in the fire and listening to the prayers, the Arhuaco man, who actually had his eyes closed, pointed his arm up to the sky. We all looked up.

He was pointing to a huge eagle floating above our ceremony, about a hundred feet in the air. It was not moving a single feather and seemed to be fixed motionless in space. It remained motionless for over ten minutes, and then the eagle floated off to the side a few feet and continued to watch us as we performed a ceremony that had not been performed for a very long time.

Don Alejandro's wife Elizabeth translated his words into English as he spoke: He sometimes spoke about things that only those present can know. One of those things is the ceremony itself. He described the ceremony in great detail, but I will keep this part mostly quiet. But we will let you hear Don Alejandro speak whenever we can.

Don Alejandro began to speak:

In the name of the heart of the heavens, and the heart of the Earth, the heart of the air, the heart of the water, in this day of today, this day is thirteen-three in the Maya calendar, which means it's the day of the authority. This ceremony is for everyone, and for all of us here present. Each one of you came with a concern or a desire, a petition. Each one of us has our own needs. And it is these needs, which make us come together and come to share with the Mayan culture here.

Here Don Alejandro began to create the Mayan ceremonial firepit. Toward the ending of building the sacred bundle, he began to explain the meaning of four of the geometrical designs.

Now the other four glyphs, in each one of the quarters, that one is symbolizing the four prophets or teachers who came from the constellation of stars, who are the ones who brought this tradition and also the ones who taught us how to do this ceremony. They lived here for hundreds of years, and they have returned to the constellation of the stars. But during that time, the time that they were here, they left us, among other things, a great prophecy, and the one prophecy that is based on that one is that we all are here together.

The star people said to us, "Children, don't forget us, keep us alive in your memories. We have given you good teachings and a healthy way of thinking. Teach it to your children and to the children of your children." And up until now, you know, it is very alive among us.

This you will not find in any book. This is transmitted alive. And this is the great mystery about the Maya, because this was transmitted in an oral way, from mouth to ear, from our ancestors.

Then, when the first ceremony happened, when the elders were here from the constellation of the stars, when they were waiting for the Sun, and they were preparing to do the first ceremony, Palenque, one of the prophets, this is what he gathered to give to us a thank you. Each one of them, they gathered sap from trees.

The second prophet brought the sap from the quill palm. They used this one to pay for when they saw the Sun for the first time, and they were able to see the beauty of the day. So then they would also pay with that another type brought from the coca palm. This is the one, and it also comes from trees. When the invasion came 500 years ago, just trying to deceive us, they started using this in the Catholic Church.

All this was taught to us by the four prophets who came from the constellation of the stars. At the time that they did the first ceremony, before the Sun appeared over the face of the Earth, they went to a mountain that is called [we will hide the name]. They started to do the ceremony, and they were asking, for they wanted to see the beauty of the day.

And suddenly a light appeared, coming from up above, that illuminated all the area where they were. Then, when the light came down, it manifested a personage within it. It was a personage full of light. The elders were placed just like we are [in a circle]. And this personage spoke to them, and he said, "My children, thank you for doing this for me. Teach it to your children and to the children of your children. In here you will find health and happiness."

They were astonished, and they were listening, and this personage was dressed with a white tunic and he had a long white beard. And one of them asked this, "But Grandfather, who are you?" And he responded, "I am the heart of the heavens. I am the heart of the Earth. I am the heart of the air. I am the heart of the water."

And he continued praying: "The Earth is yours. Populate it. Cover it." And he disappeared into the heavens again. It was at that moment that our ceremony was received by our Creator who was presented in the personification. This was done before the Sun appeared on the face of the Earth. So everything that we put here, like what they did in those days, in that day, it was an offering to our Creator. And remember that he said two things, "In here you will find health and happiness."

So on the day of today, we are doing this offering also, for it is my wish that you all do it from your heart, because this, it wasn't learned from any books. This wasn't taught by any particular person, any, just anybody. He was the Creator who came down and said, "Thank you, my children, for doing this for me." So we are doing the ceremony today.

For us this is the most sacred part, because this is the spirit of our culture. And that's when they said, this is what I tell you, "Our Creator is with us." They said, "We don't see it, but he is here with us." And that's what I say, let's do it with our hearts open. And I only say one more thing, and that is thank you for being here with us. And let's hope that the days that we are together and the days you are traveling here, the Creator be with you always, and that all your petitions will come true."

Drunvalo Continues

The prayers, the songs, the chanting, the dancing, the fire, the smoke rising to heaven, where hopefully the intentions would be heard by our Mother and Father—our hearts were wide open. It was incredible, this whole experience.

As we climbed into the boats to return to the other side of the lake, I watched as our uncommon group walked down the pier: Muslims, Jews, Buddhists, Christians, Taoists, Shinto, Hindus, and many more. All mixed in were people of the ancient tribes from Atlantis and the land of the Lotus.

Don Alejandro and the Mayan elders were looking for something—I knew this in my heart. And whatever it was, they must have found it during this ceremony, for they asked us to do another ceremony in a place a great distance from Lake Attila. The location was Tikal, an ancient temple site in Guatemala that represented the crown chakra in the human body, the entryway into higher consciousness.

Chapter Four

THE TIKAL CEREMONY

Tikal is a majestic world of primary temples that once had a city around them that extended for tens of miles in all directions. This huge city probably housed hundreds of thousands of Maya at one point. I remember looking at an artist's depiction of the city that approximated what the city might have looked like at its peak. It looked like a city of the far distant future, not from the past.

The Maya say that before they settled in Atlantis, they lived in the stars. The discovery of ancient Tikal in the 1980s revealed a resplendent city of power and beauty. You might just believe that its creators did originate in the stars if you could see their city as it was long ago.

I joined Don Alejandro, the Mayan elders, and representatives from religions and tribes around the globe in Tikal for another landmark ceremony.

We followed Don Alejandro and the Mayan elders as they moved quickly up to a high place where ceremony had obviously been performed countless times before. Again the Maya slowly and tediously began to re-create the structure of the Mayan fire ceremony. As before, it took over an hour just to construct the basic ceremonial altar, even before the fire was lit.

Tikal

At first this seemed to be a repeat of the first ceremony. But slowly, the atmosphere began to change. We were cradled in these beautiful enormous trees with huge tangled roots, and every time Don Alejandro raised his arms up to

THE MAYAN OUROBOROS

the sky, the wind blew through the trees and around us. It was pretty dramatic. After he did this about ten times, we began to expect it: if he put his arms up, we would just wait for the wind to blow.

Then the light began to change. Dramatic beams of light cut through the branches of the trees, making it feel like we were in an ancient European cathedral. Tourists who were milling by the site found that they were so mesmerized, they couldn't leave.

Again, Don Alejandro's wife Elizabeth began to translate his words to us.

When we get together in council, we always sit in the form of a circle. With this circle, and its length is about 5,200 years, we can talk about the whole history of time.

When we start counting, we count from one to twenty. And those twenty come from the five fingers of the hand or the ten fingers of both hands and the ten toes. So the twenty is equal to one person, you'd say, and this is symbolizing the zero. So a zero is a symbol of twenty.

You come here, but you don't come here to learn about being separated from each other or to learn about racism. No, we come here to learn more of what is brotherhood or sisterhood. And we give you this message, it's a message from our ancestors, just talking about or letting you know how the time is at this moment.

And through the sacred fire, because right there is the spirit of our culture. And this is what comes to nourish you, to each one of us. But this is not amusement. This is for you to take a drop of wisdom in your minds and in your souls.

So this is the world that we are living now. Because the time has come when we have to talk about these messages. Now there are messengers, traveling through all corners of the world. The messengers are troubled, and all over the world, some come from the north, some come from the south, they come from Europe, they come from all the continents. Everyone is traveling, carrying these messages. And we all speak about the same thing, that we are brothers and sisters. White and black. Indigenous or non-indigenous. Mayas and non-Mayas. We're all brothers and sisters. And my brother animal, my elder trees, my nation of stone, everything nourished by Grandfather Sun. And we travel, we move according to the movement of Grandmother Moon. And all the stars in the heavens, they have contact with us, all the planets and all the galaxies. And all the animals, the ones who live in the jungles, the ones who live underground, the ones who live in the waters, they are brothers too.

And during this time that we are traveling together in this pilgrimage, let's love each other like brothers and sisters. We are living under this sky of shadows and light, and with respect to Mother Earth, she's our mother. So it's been said now, my brothers and sisters. Thank you.

There was a moving beauty in this ceremony, but I felt that Don Alejandro and the elders were still watching and waiting for something. I felt it in my heart, but I couldn't say what it was. I felt that they were looking for signs—like the eagle we talked about before—that could only come from Mother Earth. No human being could make up these signs or influence the outcome. It had to come from Mother Earth.

Whatever the signs were, they must have appeared, for we were asked to continue.

The Mayan elders took us to remote Mayan temples that I had never heard of. I'd never even seen a photo of these, but once I saw them, I couldn't understand why the world hadn't known about then. They were exquisite. They held a deep power within the Earth. But we didn't connect with ceremonies. Don Alejandro only wanted us to experience them, or perhaps for the energy of these temples to experience us.

The Egyptian Point of View

I want to give an explanation of this Tikal ceremony, not from the Mayan point of view, but from the ancient Egyptian. In the last couple of days of our journey I discussed this with some of the people in our group, and I had several of them ask me if I would express this to all of you, so we all understand.

My involvement in these ceremonies stems from the fact that I came in from beyond the stars, from a world of no stars and planets, through Melchizedek Consciousness. This consciousness is formless, in an original state—it's one of many aspects of One consciousness. It came here at this particular time because of the massive transformation that is about to take place in our Universe. That's what Melchizedeks do. We are always involved when there are dimensional changes that are beyond the capabilities of the people involved to solve.

I came in through a place called the Crab Nebula, which is behind the middle star of the Belt of Orion, and from there I traveled to the Pleiades. I took a Pleiadian body and lived there for about fifteen Earth years in order to prepare for coming to Earth. From there I went to the star Sirius, specifically Sirius B third planet out, and spent a much shorter period of time there. I then went to the planet Venus for a short visit, and then to Earth. I arrived on Earth in 1840 in the fourth dimension.

I am just a baby here; my present lifetime is my second lifetime ever on Earth, whereas most of you have been on Earth for thousands of years.

When I arrived on Earth I was instructed to meet with the Ascended Masters, but there was no one on the fourth dimension. I moved up to the fifth and then to the sixth, where I found all of them but three, who were on the seventh dimension.

I was greeted by the ancient Egyptians who introduced me to the rest of the Ascended Masters on the sixth dimension. One of them was Thoth, the scribe who wrote down the histories of the ancient Egyptian world. Thoth has been alive for 52,000 years on Earth, and he's still here today. Much like Saint Germaine, who lives with the Ascended Masters on the sixth dimension, Thoth often re-creates his body and returns to the third dimension to help us in a human way. Like Saint Germaine, Thoth goes back and forth between our world and their world.

Shortly after I walked into my present body in 1972, Thoth and I met and began a long spiritual training, which took twelve years or more. At one point when I was finished with that training, I was told by my angelic guides that I had to leave Egypt's influence and go into the Yucatan, because the Maya held information that was important for the world as we make this transformation. The Egyptians only held part of the knowledge, and the Maya held the other part.

There are a few other tribes that are involved in this, going all the way from the Native Americans in the United States and Canada as far south as the Incas in Peru and the Waitaha in New Zealand.

There are three areas on Earth that hold the primary energies of the Unity Consciousness Grid; in other words, there is a male, female, and child aspect (positive, negative and neutral) to this grid. The male aspect was manifested in Egypt as it ran up the Nile, and it was all laid out in straight lines. The neutral or child aspect was located in Tibet, and the pyramids were made with crystals that created invisible structures. But the female aspect was manifested in North and South America and laid out in spirals, and the center of this female network, according to the Egyptians, was located in Uxmal in Mexico.

The reason we were going to Mexico and Tikal in Guatemala was to balance the female part of the Unity Consciousness Grid, which holds humanity's new blueprint of consciousness. The world had become so male that the Grid was not functioning correctly, and without bringing the female in to instill balance, the entire grid would fail to function. In other words, we would not be able to ascend.

There was a tiny, atom-sized place in Uxmal, an ancient Mayan city in the Yucatan, where a spiral began to come out of the Earth. That spiral was connected to the center of the Earth, and it evolved and expanded from Uxmal as it went to Labna and from Labna to Kabal. From Kabal, the spiral kept getting wider as it moved to Chitzen Itza; it got wider still as it went to Talum. From Talum the spiral continued on to Belize and then to Kahunlich, and from Kahunlich it spiraled around to Palenque until it reached Tikal in Guatemala.

The sites that the spiral visited are equal to the human chakras. Uxmal was the base, Labna was the sexual chakra, Kabal was the will-power chakra, Chitzen Itza was the heart, Talum was the throat, Kahunlich was the third eye, and Palenque was the pineal gland in the center of the head connected to the crown.

From the crown chakra was a connection to the thirteenth chakra, which resides one hand-length above the head. It was represented by Tikal in Guatemala. This chakra was the completion of the set of chakras that ran through the body, but it was also the beginning of another set of chakras that we will use after we ascend. Tikal was, from the Egyptian point of view, one of the most important places in the world.

Tikal is connected to another set of eight temples or pyramids moving in the opposite direction, counter-clockwise, relative to Mexico. Then there's another set further down as you go into Honduras and El Salvador and Nicaragua. The energy keeps moving, with spirals and temples that keep shifting in opposite directions each time they complete an octave. They finally enter down into Peru where the spiral changes energy and ends at a temple called Chaven. It was the spiritual center of the ancient Inca Empire.

Then at Lake Titicaca in between the Island of the Sun and the Island of the Moon, in Bolivia, deep in the waters, there's a ninety-degree turn of energy that begins to move out into the Pacific, terminating at an island called Moorea.

This same energy that moved from Uxmal in Mexico south into Guatemala and Peru and eventually reached Moorea also moves north from Uxmal in a huge half-circle into the United States and then to Hawaii and finally terminates in Moorea. Both the north and south energy lines originate in Uxmal and both come together in the little island of Moorea, which is the South Pole of the axis of the Unity Consciousness Grid. Again, this is according to the Egyptians.

Thoth sent me to Mexico and Guatemala in 1985 to put very specific kinds of crystals at each one of several sacred places. They had to be located in very precise places—they could not just be placed anywhere.

The crystals were connected to their temple and to the Earth. I put the eighth crystal at what is now called Temple Four in Tikal. In 1985, this site was almost completely buried with vegetation and massive roots. You would never know it was a temple. Only the very top of the temple was exposed.

My inner guidance told me where the sacred point was, and so we placed the crystal there. These crystals had intentions in them, and the intentions were for the grid around the world to be balanced and to come alive. There was also placed into the crystals the intention, specifically, that the Maya remember their ancient knowledge and wisdom. I received the guidance to place this intention from the Egyptians.

In 2002 the Itza Mayan Council of Elders invited me to come with another world group to the Yucatan in Mexico to be part of a series of ceremonies that were connected to the energy fields of a vast number of other tribes in North, Central and South America. Remember, the Serpent of Light, the kundalini of the Earth, had just moved from Tibet to Chile in South America, and ceremony had to be completed. In the summer of 2003, it became a reality.

Hunbatz was leading this entire complex of people and instructed our group to go to each one of these places:

Uxmal, Labna, Kabal, Chitzen Itza, Talum and Kahunlich and Palenke, to complete the cycle of what we had accomplished in 1985. We had been to all of these temples before, but it needed to be done again with the energy of many other tribes. And of course, it was all about timing.

When our group of sixty people arrived in Mexico and we connected with the Itza Council at Chitzen Itza, there were over 80,000 people watching as we performed ceremony. And to see over 250 tribes besides the Maya giving ceremony together created images that will remain with me for the rest of my life. Such power!

Our group was in the exterior of this inner circle of indigenous elders in ceremony, as we were making a wide circle around the outer edge. It was a circle within a circle, just as the Mayan Long Court moves within the Precession of the Equinox. At the end of this ceremony we all came together from different directions at the perfect moment, just as it will be on December 21 and 22, 2012.

I completed the ceremonies in Mexico, but the last temple of Tikal required traveling to Guatemala and the Maya didn't leave time for that. I was missing one temple to complete my part of the ceremony, and for the world, this was essential. Somehow, I had to make this up.

The excavation of Tikal had not been finished, and since then, the Unity Consciousness Grid above the Earth was about to be born. There's only one tiny detail left and it's complete, and that detail cannot take place until this ceremony in Tikal takes place, which completes the one at Temple Four that was supposed to be finished a long time ago. And then it's done. From an Egyptian point of view, this ceremony was so important. Without it, the Egyptians believe that all life on Earth would be extremely compromised. And from the Melchizedek Consciousness way of seeing, we also believe how crucial these ceremonies are, but only the Maya can do these ceremonies, no one else, though others may work with them. We also agree, as Don Alejandro agrees, that the ceremonies needed to have a world circle of people from all of the continents, because these are ceremonies for the world, not just the Maya. The completion of this Mayan ceremony here at Tikal allows for the completion of the Unity Consciousness Grid around the world. So you can see why this Tikal ceremony is essential.

And my heart is so thankful to Don Alejandro, I can't tell you. I'm so grateful.

This leads to the Itza Mayan Council of Elders and their belief that we should not celebrate on December 21, 2012. They believe that we should only perform ceremony to complete the blueprint of the Universe, which is absolutely required.

(12-22-2012) = 2222

On December 22, 2012, the new female cycle of creating the world will begin. This day is not only the ceremony of birth and joy, but it is the day every single person on Earth, the good and the bad, will begin a new cycle—2222. And this new cycle of 12,812.5 years (or times the Earth moves around the Sun) will begin on that day with a shorter cycle of healing. We must recover from the ending of the last cycle.

Please know that the positive result of the last cycle was not easy, but we made it, and we are here now at one of the most important moments in the history of the Earth—a moment when great change can take place.

It will be the beginning of the time, usually within a few years, when the women of the world will come together in their hearts and take control. It will not matter what country they are from, what color their skin is, what religion or spiritual belief they follow—they will become One. And this will bring in their entire families. And this will bring in the whole Earth.

It has always been this way—the male leads for half the cycle of the Precession of the Equinox, as it has the last 12,812.5 years, and then the female leads. In 12,812.5 years the female will become convoluted and distorted, just like the male is now, and the male will again take control and with youth in its veins will again lead the world.

The cycle never ends, but it is constantly changing. It's not just moving around in a circle, but the Earth is moving through space, which turns the circle into a spiral. Though the laws are the same, this allows for evolution. This is Nature's way of keeping the balance of life.

Chapter Five

THE CANDELARIA
CAVE CEREMONIES

After seventeen years of ceremony, all of the sacred components were finished and, for the Guatemala Council, the sacred signs from Mother Earth had been received to allow them to proceed deeper with our world group. Now something was possible that could not take place before.

Just after we had finished the second sacred Mayan ceremony in Tikal, Guatemala, Don Alejandro raised his arms and said, "Okay, now we're going to go to the heart of the Mayaland."

Whatever that meant, I didn't know. We began to travel in one of those huge silver tourist buses. It was sliding down the highways, moving through the beautiful jungles of Guatemala, but we didn't know where it was going. We drove for hours and hours to this unknown location, and finally, I fell asleep. I remember the rhythm of the wheels slapping on the pavement, and that was it—I began to dream.

Suddenly, without notice, Don Alejandro ordered the bus off to the side of the road. I woke up and looked outside. I saw a landscape that could have been anywhere in Guatemala. Fields of grass on both sides, fenced in by rusty barbed wire—no temples, no nothing. We all got out of the bus, kind of meandering around like a bunch of ants, not knowing what to do or where to go.

Finally Don Alejandro and the elders walked over to the other side of the road where there was a break in the fencing that led into a narrow corridor between two larger fields. There was a little space in the middle of perhaps thirty feet. If you had driven by it, you wouldn't have seen it.

We followed the Mayan elders into this narrow grassy pathway and walked for about a mile or so. The landscape became rockier, and it was clear that we were approaching some kind of low mountains. The trees began to surround us and became dense as the jungle slowly crept in.

The elders turned sharply to the left and entered into another fenced area that quickly emerged as true jungle. The blue sky began to disappear for the trees. The energy changed from ordinary to a feeling of great spiritual clarity. We all became excited with a sense of something about to happen. Mother Earth was all around us, and she was looking us straight in the eye.

As soon as I felt Mother, the jungle began to change in ways that at first seemed quite strange. Some plants looked like they had been cared for by human hands! It soon became obvious that we were approaching civilization. It was just too beautiful. But how could that be if we were moving into deep jungle?

Brightly colored birds flew back and forth as we gawked at the lushness of our surroundings. Stepping-stones appeared just when we needed them. Everything became moist, green, and carefully loved. And there it was.

The Maya had built a small place for people to prepare to enter into the caves. It was so beautiful. It looked like a flower growing out of the jungle, like something alive.

The Mayan complex blocking the entrance to the Caves

At the same time, it acted as a gate to keep out those who were not supposed to be there. It blocked the trail completely.

We had encountered a structure built by the Maya to protect something that we were about to be allowed to enter into. These were the caves from which the Maya emerged out into this world long before Atlantis. To the Native Americans, it is called the "see-pa-poo," and is the holiest of holies. To the Maya, it is the place of the birth of the Mayan Nation on Earth. Today it is called the Candelaria Caves.

The elders guided us around the backside of this alluring place to let us rest and eat. We would be in the caves for several hours. I felt myself become very quiet inside. People were talking, and I realized that food was about to be given to us. But I didn't really feel hungry. The intrigue of what lay on the other side of this open-air secret restaurant was almost unbearable.

The elders had gathered us together in this beautiful structure with the tropical jungle touching our hearts and bodies for other reasons, too. There were old Maya there, and they were feeling who we were in our hearts. It felt as if the jungle was also searching within us to see who we were.

With their graceful hospitality, the Mayan elders gave us a traditional meal, for we had a long journey ahead of us. We didn't know that, but the elders did. After lunch, we began to move single file up a slope as we approached the mountain in front of us. I became even more still inside and began to chant as I walked closer and closer to something that I didn't understand, but that my heart could feel.

And then it happened: a small hole in the side of the mountain became visible. People started talking more loudly. I could see that it was under a small ledge, an opening maybe big enough for two or three people to enter at the same time.

It took a while, but eventually all of us were inside the mountain in a long, relatively straight narrow tunnel about two meters wide. We were completely inside Mother Earth.

After walking for a few minutes in this totally dark tunnel with only flashlights to shed light, Don Alejandro corralled us all together to explain some of the basics about hiking in this cave.

He told us that this was a very sacred cave to the Mayan Nation. It continued for twenty-eight kilometers into the Earth, but we were only going to go in a few kilometers. He encouraged us to be very careful, as it would be getting wet and slippery inside. This was already obvious, but we didn't know there was a small river ahead.

We had walked just a bit farther when before us was something I didn't anticipate at all. The narrow tunnel came to an end in a T, and from about thirty feet above the floor of this new cave, we could see in front of us another enormous opening. I mean, it was twice as big as a football field, and perhaps seventy-five, maybe ninety feet high. A piece of the ceiling had fallen in long ago and a narrow beam of light came shooting into the darkness, flooding this mammoth cave with angelic light that forced you to stop and feel your heart open. You couldn't help it; it was instinctive.

Then my body came back to the reality of standing on the edge of a cliff in total darkness. I took a deep breath, and we climbed down an old hand-carved ladder to the floor of this new cave and turned to the left. When I reached the ground, I felt a slight shiver run through my body as I knew I was on solid earth. Then we continued along a small creek that weaved itself from one side of the cave to the other. We were constantly walking through pure, pristine water.

Most of the time, as we left the shaft of light, we had to use our flashlights to keep from falling into hidden rocks or off of cliffs in the dark. Most of us kept talking, simply because we wanted to make sure somebody was there. If you turned off your light it was completely black; you couldn't see a wall in front of your face.

After a very long and somewhat dangerous journey into Mother Earth, we came to another place where the ceiling had fallen out of the roof of the cave and exposed another beam of Sunlight to the interior. It wasn't much, but nevertheless, it made it possible for us to see. Don Alejandro stopped us and said that another ceremony had to be performed at this place.

The first ceremony in the caves

Again, a fire ceremony was chosen, but it was completely different than the two we had done at Lake Attila and Tikal. This was the most beautiful ceremony of all. The fire itself was in the form of an outer circle. Some of us began to play flutes and soft drums, and the music and chanting just echoed off the walls and within our spirits. My body was breathing in the holiness of the moment, but my heart was vibrating with the Universe. I found my breathing becoming rhythmic and slowing down.

Whatever happened in this ceremony was to determine our fate, though I didn't realize this at the time. We were either to stop and turn back, or, depending of the signs from Mother Earth, go deeper into her womb.

When the ceremony was over but the smoke was still rising to the ceiling, Don Alejandro disappeared. It was one of the Mayan elders, Rafino, who asked us to continue with him into the cave and who then led us deeper into our Mother's body.

For a third time, after another long, wet walk, we entered into a part of the cave system where a piece of ceiling had fallen in, and another beam of Sunlight revealed a roundish room. It was huge, but it felt cozy at the same time. Giant rocks were scattered all over the cave floor, and when we were sitting among them, we felt like we were in a smaller, more intimate space.

These rocks made me and others feel peculiar. I looked around to the woman who was standing next to me, and she appeared to be deeply concerned about what she was seeing. She said to me, "Drunvalo, look at these rocks! They look like animals and birds! These rocks look like they're alive!" I looked carefully at one that was near me, and she was right. It looked as if a really talented artist had carved a six-foot iguana into the rock. The iguana looked real, right down to the tiny details.

The large rock underneath it hid the shape of a gorilla, and the rock next to it appeared to be a young male monkey. On the walls were human faces, Mayan faces, that seemed to be emerging right out of solid rock. Every rock was alive with some life form. It took my breath away. I didn't know what to say to my friend.

I responded by saying, "Really, this is very unusual." But I felt what she was feeling—that this was not normal reality where we were standing. There was an energy there that permeated the very air we were breathing.

Abruptly, I stopped thinking about the life-forms and the energy when I noticed that Don Alejandro, who had disappeared after the last ceremony, was now sitting on a small granite ledge fifteen feet up the side of a cave wall. My first thought was, "How did he get up there?" It seemed impossible. At that moment other members of the group were becoming aware that Don Alejandro was observing us.

We became quiet, waiting for Don Alejandro to speak. One man was softly drumming as if to present Don Alejandro to the stone life-forms that were coming out of the walls, and he seemed to take heed of the cue. His words felt like they were coming from the strange animals and humans in the rocks.

Let the drums play. Thank you, Father in Heaven. You allowed us to come here to visit you, to admire your beauty, to admire your grandeur, to see and feel the love that is inside you and your womb. Thank you, Mother. We have come here to ask for peace, to ask for tranquility, to ask for love, love for us, love for our children, for the children of our children, for the future generations, for the entire world, for our governors, and for all the governed ones, we all are beings of equal value.

I ask you the most, Father in Heaven, for no more wars. No more nuclear testing. No more contamination of our environment. To respect our life, to respect the life of all living beings on the face of the Earth. My ancient trees are dying. My brother animals, they are finishing them. Those beautiful animals with beautiful skins, they come here, and they are trying to dance, my brothers, they all fly with beautiful feathers—let that beauty return once again. Allow my brother animals to live in the rivers and lakes and oceans. We ask you, Father in Heaven, let them return once again.

Time, we are getting close. We are entering the world of the Sun. There will be a change; then we will come to understand that we all are brothers and sisters. The human beings ask for freedom, and my brother animals, they want freedom too. Those beautiful mountains, they are the cities of my brother animals, now they are being exterminated.

What I feel the most in my soul, for more than 500 years of destruction, it will take more than a thousand years to reconstruct it. But Mother Nature is teaching us. She is showing us that brother animals are being born without fathers. And future generations will be like that, also. Even if they kill them by the millions, they will come back. We are the same; we leave our bodies under the ground or eaten up by the animals, but the Spirit reincarnates.

So we are One. A fulfillment of the prophecies from the eternal Maya. I feel very honored to see this group here. It gives me joy. You brought the Kogi and the Arhuaco from the Sierra Nevada, Santa Marta, Colombia; also brothers of the North [Grandfather Eric of the Hopi], and Europe, and Asia, and Oceania, they came too, to fulfill the Mayan Prophecy.

North of the center [Central America], make peace with the eagle of the north, with the condor of the south. We will meet with our brothers and sisters, because we are One, like the fingers of a hand.

Thank you, my brother Drunvalo, and my sister Diane. I see that your job is very tiresome; it is very hard. My brothers and sisters that I have met come to meet, like Adam and Carmen. I mention their names because I have come to know them, but now we have met with you, too. We all are brothers and sisters.

And we are here, in Mother Earth's Womb. Here is the center that the Grand Elder was looking for. And here we are.

Look at it well like this. You look from here to there; you see the mouth of a jaguar, with the mouth open. Here you can see many, many things. But we need more time to be here, like during the day, when the light comes in. Here, you will see, it's covered by animals and different figures. They are made in stone.

Thank you, my brothers and sisters.

When he was finished speaking, Don Alejandro looked down to the people directly below him and asked for Rafino to climb up to him. He did so, but only so that his head was level with the rock ledge where Don Alejandro was sitting. Don Alejandro reached into this rock ledge that was evidently filled with water and poured a handful of this water over Rafino's head. He did this three times. I had no idea why he was doing this. I just watched.

Don Alejandro pointed to one of the world group and asked them to come up to the rock, and he performed the same ceremony with him. We were all just watching, wondering what was going on, and then he asked each one of us to come up, one at a time.

At that moment, we all knew in our hearts what was happening. Don Alejandro was performing a Mayan water ceremony on each of us. We were being initiated in some way. And the energy in the room went deep inside our hearts. Whatever he was looking for from us, he must have found it. I started to cry. I couldn't help it. I looked around and almost everyone was crying. At that moment we were in and of One Heart.

Later, when we were back in a small Guatemalan town about to have dinner, Don Alejandro, his wife Elizabeth, and

Rafino were sitting at a table together, and they motioned for me to come over and sit with them. Don Alejandro looked into my eyes and said, "We have asked two other groups to come from all over the world to have this ceremony with us to complete our prophecy, but they could never pass the test that Pachamama (Mother Earth) presented to them. But I want to tell you now that this group has more than passed all of our expectations. You are the Ancestors that we have been waiting for."

I didn't know what he meant by this, but he and Rafino both began to cry. And Elizabeth, in her female strength, just looked at me and said, "Thank you. Please let all of the sacred group know that they are the Ones that we have been waiting for, and now our prophecy can be completed."

Chapter Six

THE POSITIVE SIDE OF THE MAYAN PROPHECY

The Maya see that an ancient prolonged cycle of time is coming to an end: both the 5,125-year Mayan Long Count cycle and the Precession of Equinox of 25,625 years. They predict that the old world, the one we live in now, is about to disintegrate from natural causes.

This means that everything we now know as normal will dramatically change. As discussed previously, the idea that the physical pole of the Earth's axis is going to shift and humanity will almost be destroyed has been termed the Doomsday of 2012.

There will probably be violence as we are birthed—there almost always is—but there is nothing we can do about it, as it is a natural cosmic cycle. We will survive this translation, as this part of the journey is merely the closing of our old world.

On the very next day, December 22, 2012, a new cycle will begin. And this cycle will be an extraordinary one like nothing the Maya have ever seen before.

Not long ago, I spent some time living in Colombia in the Sierra Nevada Mountains with the Kogi Mamos and the Arhuaco Mamos. The people of these tribes believe that there are nine worlds altogether, and that we are about to enter the fifth world. The Native Americans of both the United States and Canada also believe this.

While in Colombia, I said to the Kogi Mamos, "So we still have five more worlds to enter to reach the highest level of consciousness." I'll never forget what they said. One of them turned around; he looked at me for a moment, and he said, "No, you don't understand, Drunvalo. Everything in life is to achieve balance. The fifth world is in the middle of four worlds on either side. It is the perfect balance within the Universe. There is no higher world."

The Maya say something similar: that the next world, which they call the sixth Sun (based on zero starting point), is a world where humanity will reach a new level of consciousness. We will achieve this new level very, very quickly. The Maya say this new level of consciousness changes how we interpret the outer reality and alters our inner reality. We find ourselves literally babies in a beautiful new world.

As the new cycle technically begins on December 22, 2012, but which always actually manifests sometime within the *End of Time* window, duality consciousness, or good and bad consciousness, disappears, and a new Golden Mean unity consciousness replaces our old way of perceiving. The human ego no longer exists, and we see each other as parts of ourselves. We are changed forever.

With the opening of this new unity consciousness, the Maya predict that the human quarantine to the solar system that has existed for thousands of years will be lifted through cosmic grace given to us by Great Spirit. As it is lifted, humanity will realize that the stars and All Life Everywhere are intimately interconnected in living consciousness. The Maya are clear that we will be able to be anywhere in the Universe in time, space, dimension, and size. At this moment, this reality is beyond our imagination.

The Maya say that our human potential will reach levels that at this time would seem absolutely impossible for us. This new humanity will very quickly become normalized and accepted as the truth. To speak of it from a normal human perspective, the Maya predict that humankind will no longer be involved in finance, politics, war, food, oil, and other such things. We will become One with the Creator, and we will be able to manifest all things from within our hearts. We become co-creators with the Creator.

Remember this time, and remember the Maya, and know that what is coming is beautiful and sacred—something to celebrate and be grateful for. As Meher Baba once said, "Don't worry, be happy." This is definitely the best approach for life at this time. Breathe from your heart. Life is not what it seems; it's not even close to what most of our parents believed to be true. We are on the edge of a fantastic odyssey to remember ourselves.

We live in a dream that our mind has crystallized into what we call Reality. We believe it is fixed and can only change according to the laws of physics. The Maya believe you will soon know a part of yourself that is so ancient that it goes beyond the stars and planets. They are just a dream also—and just like a dream, upon waking, you realize that it was nothing but light, or better still, nothing but pure consciousness. It is a time for you to remember who you really are. This knowledge is very much alive inside your heart, and you will remember. Everything has been prepared, and our new world is now ready to receive you.

In la'Kesh.

Part II

THE BIRTH OF A
NEW HUMANITY

Chapter Seven

THE EGYPTIANS

What does it mean that everything has been prepared?

Winged Maat

To jar your ancient memory a little, I'm going to tell you a long, beautiful story about something that hardly anyone knows about on Earth today, but which has a direct effect upon every last person on Earth, including you.

The story is based upon the Mayan Precession of the Equinox of 25,625 years and the Mayan Long Count of 5,125 years. We've touched on these before, but instead of viewing these stories from a Mayan perspective, we will see them through the eyes of the ancient Egyptians. We are doing this because the Egyptians were the creators of the events in this story and only they truly can tell it.

The events of this story have been successfully hidden from the world for thousands of years, but the Ascended Masters know everything about this subject, and there are others. There are secret groups within the Tibetan Buddhists, the Sufis, some of the Masons, and a few groups in Hinduism, but the large religious groups have no idea what we are talking about here, and most of the ordinary world doesn't have a clue.

Science is just beginning to understand. Because this is something that you may not know, you will have to hang in there with me. This is not something that you learned in school, even though it is just now being accepted by scientists.

In your heart you already know this information, and you know it very, very well. It's just that you have forgotten what it is. And so everything we are about to speak about is not meant to teach you, but rather to trigger your own memories. You have lived through this in ancient times, and you know what we are talking about. Please keep that in mind, and allow yourself to be able to make changes within yourself as you hear these words—otherwise you're really going to miss the deep, secret aspect of what is intended.

The Forgotten History and the Human Unity Consciousness Grid

The story began in a land called Atlantis. Yes, I know that scientists are not certain that Atlantis ever existed, even though people in history like Plato of Ancient Greece said that it did. There is no definitive evidence to prove that it actually sank below the ocean waves. But there are remnants of people who are still alive today who do remember.

The Hopi of Arizona, USA do remember, and they have told me personally that they used to live on Atlantis. The Kogi and the Arhuaco say the same thing. I even met a Mongolian shaman who said that his tribe remembers that they used to live on Atlantis. They even remember exactly how they traveled from Atlantis to Mongolia. The people who remember keep these memories hidden in their stories they tell their children and in the hearts of their shamans.

And then there were the Maya, who also tell me they used to live in Atlantis. To back them up, there is documentation from the discovery of several Mayan stones found in one temple in the Yucatan that the Maya used to live in Atlantis thousands of years ago. The Mayan Stones are called the Troano Document (part of the Madrid Codex), and they are currently located in the Museo de América in Madrid, Spain.

These stones show an ancient city in Atlantis, and how, on a single day, the Earth began to move and volcanoes started exploding. The Maya got into boats and rowed from where they were in Atlantis to the present-day Yucatan in

Mexico. The Southwest of Atlantis was not far away from that area, and it was completely reasonable for them to row to safety and find that location.

We do have living people who remember ancient Atlantis, and it is from these modern tribes and the ancient Egyptians that we are drawing most of this information.

The time of Atlantis was a point in history when humans had developed consciously to a very high level—a level of consciousness beyond anything that we assume is even possible for humankind. But we were there. We had broken the bonds of gravity, our bodies were able to levitate, and we were able to move in space vehicles and explore the solar system. Like I said, it's hard to believe.

However, only fewer than a thousand people had actually reached that stage of evolution. Most of the ordinary people of Atlantis were in a level of consciousness similar to what we are in now in the twenty-first century, and in between those people and these very high-level beings were the Maya.

The Maya were the translators between the people with this very high level of consciousness, who were called the Nakkals, and the ordinary people of Atlantis. The Nakkals lived in totally dark pyramids, floated a few inches off the ground, and glowed in the dark, lighting up the pyramids. They were the living dreamers who created outer reality from dreams from their hearts. The Maya were the priesthood, the ones who translated through ceremony what was being told to them by this inner group of very high beings to the ordinary people in Atlantis.

Everything was going fine for thousands of years, until about 4,000 years before the sinking of Atlantis. A meteorite came out of the night sky and struck the Earth, just missing the western shores of Atlantis, which would be now very close to the eastern shores of the United States. Before it hit the ocean, it broke into three pieces.

The three pieces went into the ocean and made three huge, deep holes near the edge of Atlantis. And the meteorites rained smaller pieces all over the eastern shores of what would someday become the Eastern United States. To this day these meteorite fragments can be found in many of the southeastern states.

One of the three pieces of the meteorite struck very close to Atlantis and destabilized their continent. It left them on the edge of a huge abyss. And so, 4,000 years later, or a little less than 13,000 years ago from now, Earth experienced a pole shift. The continent of Atlantis couldn't withstand the extreme movement and being so close to this enormous hole in the Earth, it sank into the ocean.

The high-level Nakkals knew their continent was going to go underwater—they knew at least 200 years before the event—and thus they were prepared for the catastrophe.

The Mer-Ka-Ba Pyramid of Ancient Atlantis

One group of Atlantians, composed of scientists, who were perhaps misguided, built a very large pyramid made out of stone. That pyramid sits off the coast of Bimini, down deep into the ocean. Modern scientists have discovered this pyramid and the underwater roads that lead to it and are attempting to use this evidence to prove the existence of Atlantis. It was this pyramid that is the source of most of the present-day chaos our world is now experiencing.

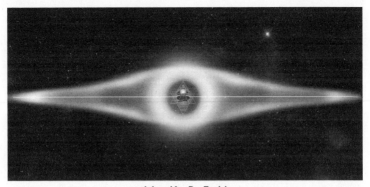

Mer-Ka-Ba Field

This group of seven scientists built this pyramid for an explicit purpose: to create a Mer-Ka-Ba Field. The Mer-Ka-Ba is normally thought of as the human body light body's, but the blueprint of this energy field can also be used synthetically to power a spaceship or even in a building such as a pyramid.

Their purpose was self-centered. They wanted to control the continent of Atlantis and eventually the entire world. But it had been over 50,000 years since they had actually attempted to create a Mer-Ka-Ba Field, and so they didn't really know exactly how to do it, and they lost control of this experimental Mer-Ka-Ba.

What took place was horrible. The Mer-Ka-Ba contains the blueprint of the Universe, and it split open the levels between the third and the fourth dimensions. It exposed human beings to a level of consciousness and awareness that they were not prepared for, and it forced beings from other levels of existence to enter the third dimension on Earth. These beings had no choice but to enter into human bodies to survive, which meant that almost everyone on Atlantis became possessed.

It was ugly and painful for both sides, and it ended up being a disaster on a level humanity has never experienced in modern times. World War II was nothing compared to this. So for the last couple hundred years of Atlantis, people were sick and dying and infested with these other-world beings.

The Nakkals and the Ascended Masters decided that they had to do something. They went into a conscious connection with the center of our own galaxy and received permission to do something that is very rare. Since we had already reached this high level of consciousness, and we had obtained it naturally, Galactic Command made a decision and gave permission for Earth to reestablish the Unity Consciousness Grid that was destroyed when the dimensions were separated so that humans would eventually be able to again reach this high level of consciousness.

Before the Fall

The Nakkals and the Ascended Masters knew that we were going to fall, and they chose three of their members to lead a risky experiment. They had nothing to lose—if they did nothing, mankind would have to begin all over again, and it would take at least 200,000 years to return to the levels we had reached.

Three men became paramount in this whole story. These three men engineered and conceived of a plan to bring us humans back into higher consciousness.

Their names were Chequetet Arelich Vomalites, Ra, and Araragat, and they were all Ascended Masters. They were immortal beings who worked through the Nakkals. In fact, all of the Nakkals were Ascended Masters who chose to remain on Earth in physical form.

What these three men decided to do was something that had rarely been tried in the Universe before. They began this process of returning our consciousness to us by building a structure out in the middle of nowhere. They chose this place for a very specific reason, which I will talk about a little while later. It was the place that we now call Egypt, and this building was the Great Pyramid of Giza.

The pyramid was constructed before the sinking of Atlantis. The three had to manifest it first, because it was more than just a building—it was a global landmark.

The Great Pyramid at Giza

According to Chequetet Arelich Vomalites, the Great Pyramid at Giza was built through consciousness, not physical labor, in a matter of hours. Even more crazy, it was built from the top down.

When I presented this information to the Egyptian government back in the nineties, they thought I was crazy, too. But they had their scientists check it out to know for certain.

They carbon-dated the mortar in between the stones, from the top to the bottom, and found out that the oldest stones were on the top and the youngest ones were on the bottom. They couldn't explain it. They couldn't contradict what I was saying. Of course, since they couldn't explain it, they stopped talking about it.

Now, to understand this a little bit further, it wasn't just from this one pyramid that the three were going to bring back our consciousness. That was just the beginning. The original plan included a web of pyramids, sacred sites, and what would in the future be churches, mosques, synagogues, and temples from all religions on Earth. It was a web of these structures and natural landmarks from all over the Earth, approximately 83,000 of them, that would be built over about 13,012.5 years (12,812.5 plus 200) that would construct a global geometrical electromagnetic energy field that would surround the Earth. It was through this energy field that these three ancient men were constructing that we would regain our higher consciousness (or from our point of view, ascend).

What's so interesting about these structures is that they were built over almost 13,000 years, but the entire structural plan was created in a matter of hours—not on this dimension, but on the fourth dimension, on the higher frequencies of the Earth's consciousness. The entire structural plan was created through consciousness, in the same way they built the Great Pyramid, from the top down. Once these buildings were created on the fourth dimension, the three men slowly began to pull them out of the fourth dimension into this third dimension, which took thousands of years.

The physical pyramidal system was built by ancient tribes and cultures around the world. A good example is the pyramids of the Yucatan in Mexico. They were built by the Maya, but the Ascended Masters orchestrated their construction. And the construction of this consciousness grid has been directed through all these thousands of years up to this very minute as you are reading this book by these amazing men and women who have taken the very spiritual path you are on now.

Like you are about to do, they mastered their lives, overcame death, and in a flash of light, they became immortal. The Ascended Masters are our ancestors who in their wisdom are watching over us, slowly leading us into a higher manner of perceiving the Universe. The Ascended Masters directed the building all over the world; for example, of the hundred massive pyramids running down the islands of Japan. This was the beginning of something, an ancient science, which in our modern world we know only a little bit. It's a science called geomancy.

Geomancy

What were the ancient cultures doing by building these pyramids and temples all over the world, and how could creating stone buildings create a field of energy above the Earth?

Well, it was a very advanced level of what today, in modern times, we call geomancy. Geomancy is a modern term—I am sure they had another name for it in Atlantis.

I would personally define geomancy as the use of stones, rocks, crystals, or metals to change the energy flow of the Earth. We do this with our computers; we control the flow of electricity with objects such as diodes and capacitors; but it can also be done on a large scale, such as the Earth herself.

When these massive buildings are placed on very precise places on the Earth, they change the internal flow inside the Earth. Example of this are the Geopath Lines or the Hartmann Lines, which change the external flow above the Earth. Geopath Lines are created by such things as volcanoes and their lava flow, tectonic plate pressures, and even ocean pressure. The Hartmann Lines are a natural flow of energy that is in a grid line pattern covering most of the Earth.

I mentioned that I would talk again about where the Great Pyramid was built on the Earth. The ancient Egyptians somehow managed to calculate the exact center of the landmass of the Earth. When a building like the Great Pyramid is placed in the exact center of the landmass of the Earth, it holds a pivotal position that can change the flow of energy within and above the Earth. When 83,000 other global sites are specifically connected to the Great Pyramid and it functions as a whole unit, things are possible that would normally seem like miracles.

The Egyptians were creating a new Unity Consciousness Grid—the exact natural grid that we lost in Atlantis. Remember, the destruction of that grid caused the fall of humanity into the darkness and density of the Modern World. This is the same "fall" mentioned in the Christian Bible.

And this same grid will be our salvation from darkness back into the light. In order for us to rise back into higher consciousness, we must have this grid. The Ascended Masters are making certain that we will join them again. You are their Solar Brother or Sister, and they will never stop assisting you until you can exist on the plane of pure light. Without this Unity Consciousness Grid around the Earth, we are quarantined to this third dimension and kept separate from the rest of life. We cannot return to the freedom of our higher consciousness. It's impossible.

Human Extinction?

One hundred and twelve years ago, at the birth of the twentieth century, scientists believed there were approximately thirty million species of living forms on Earth. It took about 4.6 billion years, depending on who you talk to, for those thirty million species to develop by the beginning of the twentieth century.

But in the last 112 years, because of the drop in our collective consciousness, we have rapidly destroyed most of these living species with our human actions. We are now down to approximately fourteen to fifteen million species on Earth and falling daily. Every single day new species become extinct. It appears that over half of the life that's on Earth is now extinct; it's gone, to never to be seen again, probably.

If we can make it into the next level of existence, all of this will end. We will be able to fix what took place over this last 112 years. If we do not return to this higher level of consciousness, one of two things is going to take place, and almost all of the indigenous tribes that I've talked to around the world agree.

If we do not make it back to this level of consciousness that we had achieved before, we will end up killing this planet and all life on it, including humanity. We will destroy this dear Earth.

If we are successful, and I feel certain we will be, life will continue not only for humanity, but for all life on this planet.

Consciousness Grids

Each of the thirty million species has to have a geometrical electromagnetic field that extends around the entire Earth—a consciousness grid—in order for them to exist on Earth. Each one of these consciousness grids is absolutely unique, just like snowflakes.

The geometry of each species' unique grid reflects exactly the geometry, shape, and form of the life form's physical body. You could tell very quickly that an insect, for instance, came from a particular geometry.

Of these fourteen or fifteen million consciousness grids that are left on Earth today, three are human. This means we actually have three different kinds of human beings on Earth. Each one perceives reality in a different way.

The Aboriginal Grid

The first one is the Aboriginal Grid, which represents the original people on Earth, like the Aboriginals in Australia. There are little pockets of these kinds of people around the world that are still functioning on the original grid that preceded modern humanity.

If you ask an Aboriginal from Australia to look at a photo, he will only see colors and shapes, but he will not be able to actually see the photo. It is because Aboriginals really do have a different consciousness than ours.

Little is known about the Aboriginal Consciousness Grid. It was the first human grid, and scientists don't know what it looks like geometrically, or even its basic shape.

The Modern Grid

The Rhombic Triacontahedron around the earth

About the second human grid, which maps the industrial world's level of consciousness, we know quite a bit. This grid is believed to be a rhombic triacontahedron, which is a very specific relationship between an icosahedron and a pentagonal dodecahedron.

This grid surrounds the world, and has places where the lines cross or intersect that relate to specific areas on the surface of the Earth. It was the United States, we believe, that first discovered that this electromagnetic grid spanned the world, though Russia also had something to do with its discovery. It's very interesting that most of the military bases in the world between Russia and the United States are located exactly on those nodal points.

Why would they do that? Because they both knew that this second grid was the consciousness grid of most of the planet's population, and they believed if they could control this grid, they could control most of the people in the world. It's an obvious military move to make, and they've known this for a very long time now. I think it went back into probably the '60s when they first discovered this information.

The Unity Consciousness Grid

The Unity Consciousness Grid

This is the third human grid, the one that Chequetet Arelich Vomalites and Ra and Araragat are creating by making sacred sites all around the world and performing specific geomancy. The grid is slowly formed around the Earth, every time the three build a new site. Each new pyramid or temple changes the shape of the grid above the Earth a little bit. They keep getting it closer and closer to a grid that is also an icosahedron-pentagonal-dodecahedron blend, different than the Modern Grid, perfectly positioned at a very specific angle.

The Unity Consciousness Grid was discovered by Russia. I'm sure they have conducted massive research on how the grid relates to the next level of human consciousness, because that's where we're going and the Russians know this. The Russians know more about these kinds of things than anyone, I believe.

Without the Unity Consciousness Grid, you could become an Ascended Master, but with limitations. You would be tied to the Earth until all humans achieved the next level of consciousness. We could not move as an entire race, as an entire planet. We cannot move until the third Unity Consciousness Grid is completed and breathing.

The Golden Mean Again

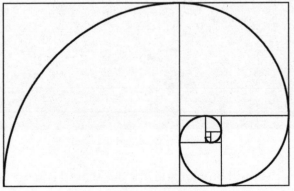

The Golden Mean with spiral

For more understanding . . .

The differences in these three consciousness grids, these three different ways of perceiving the reality, are also tied to the Golden Mean.

All of life is always trying to reach this special ratio of 1.6180339 through the Fibonacci Series, as we said before, but so is consciousness itself.

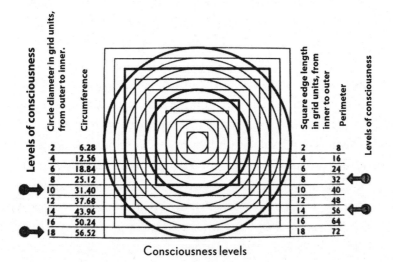

Consciousness levels

Consciousness levels are found in a relationship between the square and the circle. When the perimeter of a square and the circumference of a circle are exactly the same, the Golden Mean ratio appears. Life consciously slowly approaches the Golden Mean in stages, just as it does in body proportions, as we spoke about earlier.

The Aboriginal Grid is very close to the Golden Mean, but it's not perfect. And the Aboriginals have been in a sustainable relationship with the Earth for tens of thousands of years or longer.

The second grid, the Modern Grid, is not even close to matching the Golden Mean. The result is that we humans are not in tune with nature. This is why we are killing our planet and through our actions have reduced half of the species on Earth. We don't care.

We are meant to be a transition state between the Aboriginal state and the next level of consciousness beyond human consciousness, which we call Unity Consciousness. We are meant to be here on Earth, spend as little time as possible, and as fast as possible go on to the next level of consciousness. We are a bridge level of consciousness that takes us from one side to the other. This second grid level is a stage that must happen, but one that must be transcended quickly or we will inevitably destroy anything we touch.

The next level beyond human consciousness is more harmonic than the Aboriginal state; it is much closer to the Golden Mean ratio. And if we can just make it to that place, then we will be able to solve all of humanity's problems. From that level of consciousness, we can create anything from our heart's core, and it becomes easy to solve problems that from our present level of consciousness seem confusing and impossible.

This second grid is based on what we call polarity consciousness. It's got different names around the world, but it simply means that we see everything as either black or white, and we are constantly judging every situation. We judge every person we see as good, bad, or neutral. And this is the nature of polarity consciousness.

This type of consciousness is a problem because it creates the ego in the mind. The ego thinks only of itself; it doesn't think of other people, except for people it loves or who are close to it. It really only cares about itself. That's the level of consciousness that most of us are in now.

Normally these consciousness grids are created naturally over hundreds of thousands of years. In the course of everyday life, we slowly evolve and through our actions we begin to create the next grid of consciousness naturally. When the cycles of time are right, we move up to the next grid.

Synthetic Unity Grid

Because we had arrived at this level of consciousness once before, we're being allowed to reach this level again. However, we will reach it *synthetically*, through creating pyramids and buildings and structures and temples all over the world, not by natural means within ourselves.

This is a synthetic way of returning to our ancient level of consciousness. It is not natural, but if it works, we will return automatically to a natural pathway. Nature will then take over and bring us to even higher levels at the right time, which is contained in our DNA.

We're being given a second chance at life, but this synthetic pathway has been in place long before the beginning of our present civilization. In ancient Egypt, people built pyramids in an attempt at entering into higher consciousness. They also used frails, rods, and hooks—all physical objects that they used to put on their bodies and spines to tune them to the higher levels of consciousness. This was purely synthetic. Everything that has been going on for the last 13,000 years has been synthetic to get us to this place we are at now.

Once we have achieved unity consciousness, all of these pyramids and sacred sites will not be of any use anymore, and we will be able to go on our own, without anybody's help. We will be free. And this is also part of the Mayan Prophecy. We will reach the safety of our new consciousness, and our birth into the higher worlds will become reality. We will remember our intimate connection with Great Spirit, and from that moment on, Nature will take over.

Human History

I guess there's another little piece that we should explain. I've talked about these three men: Chequetet Arelich Vomalites, Ra, and Araragat. To be clear, I've never met Ra or Araragat. I know they are elder Ascended Masters, but the angels only wanted me to work with Chequetet.

I studied intensely with Chequetet Arelich Vomalites for about fourteen years and learned much about humanity and history. Chequetet was the King of Atlantis for a very long time. According to the Emerald Tablets, which were written 2,000 years ago by Hermes of Ancient Greece, Chequetet was an Ascended Master and had mastered death. Hermes said that Chequetet had lived as the king of Atlantis for 52,000 years, and if this were true, he would know a great deal of the history of humanity personally. He was also one of the living Nakkals. He is still alive today.

Six thousand years after Atlantis sank below the ocean, human civilization began to grow in Sumeria. A few hundred years later, Egypt was born. In this new country, Chequetet changed his name to Thoth. Thoth was not concerned with being the king of Egypt—instead, he took on the role of the scribe, the person who wrote down and recorded their history.

Thoth and Shesat as hieroglyph

Just so you understand, the angels, the original spheres of light, led me to Thoth, and pretty much everything that I have learned about the history of the Earth came from him. But not just him. Thoth was married to a woman named Shesat, and she was also the scribe of Egypt and recorded the history as she experienced it. Shesat has helped me understand history even more than Thoth.

To Thoth, men and women see and experience events differently. To truly understand what happened in any event, you must see the event from both the male and the female perspective.

I'm going to expand on this one a little, because it applies to so many other subjects. Like the reason why we have a mother and a father. Each parent sees differently, but both points of view together create a whole that is closer to the truth, and this gives the child a better chance to survive, to understand life, and to grow and reach for higher levels of consciousness.

What Thoth told me was that almost all of modern history was written by men, and the female view was not considered important. This gives a view of history that is distorted. From my point of view, the history that we know is based upon the winners of the wars, who were almost always men and who then told us what happened, but of course, only from their point of view.

This was not how things worked in Egypt. Thoth wrote down his ideas, his observations, and what he sensed, and his wife wrote down her observations, beliefs, and her sensing completely separately. They did not agree at times, but they knew that was proper for the people of the future.

Let's now look at a history of humanity that, until just recently, almost no one alive was aware of.

Chapter Eight

CARL P. MUNCK

Now we need to add another piece to all of this so it begins to have credibility. You will see that this is not just fantasy or imagination; this is hard science mathematics.

Carl P. Munck is a researcher who discovered that when you go to any of the sacred sites—pyramids, churches, and temples around the world—with a little knowledge, you will see a code written on the external face of each sacred structure.

You don't even have to go inside the structure to decipher this code. The coded information is contained in the shape, with the number of steps, and a lot of different forms on the outside of these structures. To learn more about Munck's codes, visit his website at *www.greatdreams.com/gem1.htm*. To be clear, I am only giving you a review of his work and there is much more to Munck's work than what I am covering in this book.

If you know how to read Munck's code, you will see a series of three numbers on each of the pyramids or temples around the world. These three numbers tell you exactly the temple's longitude—the same one we are using today—and an ancient calculation of latitude, which is different than what we use today.

Munck's newest work with this code will even give you the structure's altitude relative to sea level, which was very different during the time of Atlantis. How could the ancient Atlantians possibly know what the sea level would be in the twenty-first century?

Though the mathematics has not been worked out on all 83,000 sacred sites around the world, Munck has studied 250 sites, and the math is all perfect. So far, not even one sacred site is not part of this global grid.

How is it possible that an ancient culture could have the technology to accomplish this global feat? Scientists today can only imagine how to do this with our modern GPS system. Thirteen thousand years ago, in the time that our history paints as being inhabited by hairy barbarians, people were doing complex mathematical calculations.

The 6,000-year-old walls of Egypt also prove history wrong, as the ancient Egyptians showed in hieroglyphs of the Earth depicting the North and South Poles in their precise locations and in the precise shapes of the landmass and ice mass. How did they do that? We don't know how they did it, but it is fact.

Carl Munck's great work has now been introduced at the United Nations. He gave the world the entire mathematics and exactly how it works. But the United Nations had no way of integrating this new information into their understanding of history. This put the UN in a delicate position. They could not deny the facts, but they couldn't accept this truth without changing the entire world's view of history. So what did they do? They brushed it under the rug and tried to forget it like they have done with so many other world anomalies.

And so what I'd like to do now is just let you read directly from Carl's work, some of what he has found to be true, and hopefully this will make everything clearer.

Finding Hidden Numbers by Carl Munck

"How do you "hide" a number in a Sacred Site? Well, for example, in a stone circle at 49 degrees, 1 minute, 1 second of longitude, you might have 7 stones in a circle, with a stone in the center that is perfectly square: 7 squared = 49. A step pyramid at that longitude could be perfectly square at the base, with 7 tiers on each side.

This all may seem like stretching a point—until you realize that most sites have a longitude or latitude that can only be represented by very long numbers. For example, if you have a latitude of 25 degrees, 07 minutes, 29.62285728 seconds (north or south of the equator), the number you are working with, multiplied out, is 5,184. If you find that by adding and/or multiplying various measurements in a pyramid at that exact latitude, you can arrive at the number 5,184, the probability of coincidence becomes mathematically negligible. If you *also* find that the *longitude* of this pyramid can be derived in like manner, it's even less likely that you are looking at something that occurred by chance.

Going further, what if you study upwards of 250 Sacred Sites and find that the longitude relative to Giza and the exact latitude are encoded into every single one? Even if there were only ten sites involved, you would have ruled out coincidence. And Carl Munck has discovered that *you can find the exact longitude relative to Giza and the latitude, down to several decimal places, encoded into every single one of the 250 Sacred Sites that he has studied!*

In proving that the placement of the Sacred Sites could not have occurred by chance, Munck has also proved that the people who built them *must have been able to view our planet from outer space!* It would have been literally impossible for us, today, to verify the accuracy of these ancient builders' calculations before we ourselves had satellites!

So Munck is giving us proof that there was a much higher technology in ancient times than classical historians have assumed. Besides that, the overwhelming implication is that the Sacred Sites—at least the ones that Munck has visited—were planned and executed by the same mind or agency. They were all built according to a *single plan.*

Now that you've heard Munck's words, you begin to understand that there is this grid of approximately 83,000 sites all over the world that were precisely put on the planet in very specific places, and that it was not possible that this could have been designed by all these indigenous tribes like the Mayans or the Egyptians or the Chinese, especially since these people lived at different times in history. Rather, this had to be of a single mind, a single thought, a single plan. There is no other way. And this changes the whole understanding of our history and who we were before and who we are now.

The Prime Meridian

What about the Prime Meridian, the line of longitude that is positioned exact at zero degrees? Ra, Araragat, and

Chequetet Arelich Vomalites knew where the physical poles and the equator would be positioned far into the future. How they knew this Thoth never told me, but he was an Ascended Master and a fourth dimensional being. On those levels the third dimension is easy to perceive. The Prime Meridian we use today is not the one the ancients based their system on. The one that these three Ascended Masters used involves the Great Pyramid at Giza in Egypt. If you take the North Pole and the South Pole and run a line directly over the apex of the Great Pyramid, that is the Prime Meridian of the ancient system. This makes sense, as it was the first building built in the entire system.

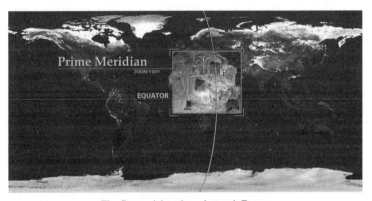

The Prime Meridian through Egypt

How was this massive energy project manifested? For these three men, it was easy. Because of their level of consciousness, they dreamed the entire project into existence on the fourth dimension and then, very slowly, they connected with different cultures or tribes on the third dimension. They would give these tribes the blueprint instructions about where to build and in what form through meditation.

Now you can see what Chequetet Arelich Vomalites, Ra, and Araragat were doing. They were creating these structures all over the world to change the internal flow of the Earth's energies, which is called geomancy, so that the external flow was altered, and in so doing, slowly creating this geometrical electromagnetic field that surrounds the Earth. And in doing that, they were re-creating our Unity Consciousness Grid that was lost in Atlantis. December 22, 2012. Super intelligence!

This was a gift of love. It shows that we are not alone in our consciousness, and that we are not forgotten. Our ancestors remember us, and they are taking care of us. These are the Old Ones who are still connected to us now. They extend through all cultures and all levels of life, even down to ordinary families around the world. These are our ancestors doing something for us so that we can make changes within ourselves that must be made. And in making these changes, we do something for them. We bring them back. A day will come in the near future when we will again meet our ancestors, for life never ever dies.

Chapter Nine

THE ATLANTIAN MEMORY LOSS AND THE RUSSIAN SPACE STATION MIR

After Atlantis sank, it took time for humanity to recover. All personal memory was lost, except for that of the Nakkals and some of the Maya. The average person had a disease similar to dementia, and could not remember anything in their lives; most people went entirely insane. They definitely couldn't build pyramids with mathematically perfect stones. The Ascended Masters had to wait until a specific time in the Precession of the Equinox when it was possible to continue. This wait was a little more than 6,400 years.

Since the average Atlantian was originally a very advanced person, but had lost his entire memory, he degraded into what seemed like a barbarian. If a modern person lost his entire memory, he wouldn't even know how to get out of a house. The Atlantians had to discover fire all over again.

This loss of memory was caused by the Earth's geomagnetic field going to zero strength just before the Earth's physical pole shift that sank Atlantis. Until recently, science had no idea that it was possible for a human being to lose all memory when the Earth's magnetic field went to zero. Note that modern-day scientists predict that the North and South magnetic poles will reverse, which means that the geomagnetic poles will go through zero.

Mir Space Station

When the Russians placed the Mir Space Station into space and the first Russian cosmonaut entered the satellite, this is exactly what happened. After about fourteen days in zero-gravity space, this Russian cosmonaut lost all of his memory, and was not able to control the Mir Space Station. The Russians immediately sent someone up to replace him and to return the first cosmonaut back to Earth.

THE MAYAN OUROBOROS

After studying this man, they found that his memory was permanently erased and he was insane. Then the Russians discovered that the same thing happened to the cosmonaut that replaced him. It was then that Russian scientists created a device to approximate the Earth's geomagnetic field around an individual that could be worn on the spacesuit. It is now understood that space travel is not possible, if it is more than two weeks long, unless the Earth's geomagnetic field is approximated within and around the space ship or at least around the individual.

Scientists have also discovered that the human brain cells have a magnetic membrane around each cell. They are studying how memory is retained within human consciousness, which does appear to be through magnetics, similar to the materials in a CD or DVD.

Obviously, a reversal of the geomagnetic field would almost certainly be followed by a space of time before the field started up again in reverse. If this time were fourteen days or more—and in cosmic time, fourteen days is nothing but a nanosecond—human memory would be lost completely. This is what happened in Atlantis, and it could again in our modern time.

The Story of the Last Ceremonies

The Maya, Hopi, Kogi, and Arhuaco all agree that there are going to be incredible Earth changes, but we have already discussed those. You are not going to have to worry about such things. You are going to ascend before the geomagnetic field reachs the critical level into another dimension of

Earth's consciousness where there is only peace. This is how this transition was meant to be experienced.

The Ascended Masters had to wait until the midpoint between the apogee and the perigee of the Precession of the Equinoxes before they could return the memories, knowledge, and wisdom to humanity, as we said before. And as we know, the pyramids and temples were built continuously around the world on the third dimension right after that midpoint, about 6,400 years ago.

Suddenly there was an explosion of earthly knowledge, and the sacred buildings began to appear around the world. Each time one of these structures was built, the Unity Consciousness Grid would begin to form a little bit closer to the proper geometrical shape and become a little closer to what would be necessary for us to connect as a living energy field. This progressed all the way up until, say, around sixty-five years ago, directly after World War II.

And then things began to happen on another level. Extraterrestrials began to become involved in humanity's actions on an accelerated level. Only one year after World War II was over, in the summer of 1946, spaceships appeared all over every single military base in Europe, almost without exception. The following year, in June of 1947, spaceships appeared all over the military bases in the United States. How do I know this? Because there are historical documents by the head of the Air Force project "Bluebook" that proves it. If you want this book, it is available at *www. drunvalo.net.*

Book by Captain Ruppelt

The appearance of the ETs opened another doorway, as they became involved in the work of this grid. By the late fifties, we began to see crop circles all over England, but in the beginning they were rather simple.

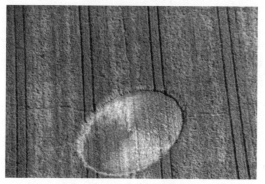

Crop circles in the 1950s

By the eighties and nineties we began to see extremely complex crop circles that baffle the mind, especially when you know they are always finished in a single night. In all the "real" crop circles, there has never been found any evidence of human involvement.

Around the turn of the century, crop circles began to be found in ice and snow, and were called ice or snow circles.

Ice/snow crop circles

Then we found crop circles in trees in Canada. The trees were grown into complex geometrical crop circles. No human being could have done this, either.

Colin Andrews, one of the world's primary crop circle researchers, discovered that about 80 percent of the crop circles were manmade. But the other 20 percent were not, for they defy all scientific explanations. These "real" crop circles grow into the geometric circles, and the crops are still alive, not pushed down with boards by human beings, which kills the plants.

These real crop circles were another level of higher communication that began to take place around the world. It was important communication to all of humanity, and hundreds of groups, individuals, and especially governments, began to try to break the code of what these crop circles were saying to us. The Russians shed some light on this subject when they recently made an interesting discovery.

Dr. Marina Popovich

Dr. Marina Popovich was a Russian who was born July 20, 1931. She is a retired Soviet Air Force colonel, engineer, and legendary Soviet test pilot who holds 107 aviation world records set on over forty types of aircraft. She is one of the most famous pilots in Russian history, and one of the most important female pilots of all time.

Dr. Popovich began research, along with other Russian scientists, on the global crop circles that have appeared in our crops for almost sixty years, searching for their origins. If they were not manmade, she figured, the communication must be buried within the geometry.

Actually, there have been hundreds of groups, and a large number of governments, that have researched the geometries and possible origins of the crop circles. Everyone understands that these crop circles probably contain communication, because the mathematics embedded within some of them were so advanced that there were only a handful of humans alive who could even understand the math. But we didn't know how or what they are saying to us until Dr. Marina Popovich released her scientific papers.

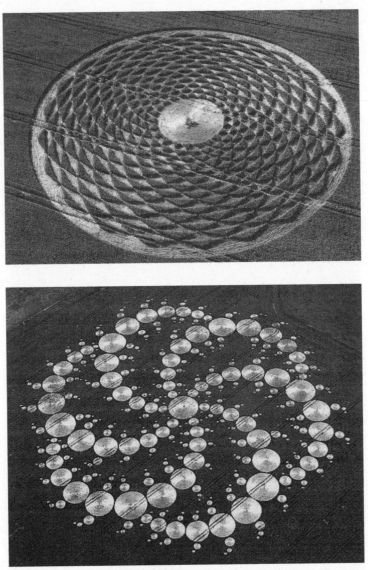

Two complex crop circles

Dr. Popovich, along with other Russian researchers, deciphered the code, and they are now able to read the crop

THE MAYAN OUROBOROS

circles like a book. This enormous discovery was backed by five eminent Russian scientists, and attracted world attention in 2011. Today there are over fifty Russian scientists and many others from around the world who support her views.

Dr. Popovich believes that these crop circles are being created by extraterrestrial civilizations (ETC) who are trying to warn humanity about catastrophic changes that are coming to the Earth very soon. The ETC say that the weakening of Earth's magnetic field has reached a critical value, and threatens the life of mankind.

Specifically, Dr. Popovich says the crop circles are saying that there will be eight catastrophes that will happen on Earth, one after another, beginning at the peak of this solar cycle number twenty-four, which is expected in mid- to late-2013.

According to the crop circles, we will most likely not even be able to survive the second catastrophe, and therefore we have to move up into higher consciousness soon, either before or directly after the first catastrophe. If we make it to this higher consciousness, all will be well. This is the primary message from the ETC in a nutshell.

The first catastrophe, as related by the Russians, will involve solar flares coming off the Sun and reaching such strong levels that the Sun erases all the computer memory banks of the world. By this we mean hard drives, CDs, DVDs, and other memory technologies based upon magnetics, except for those that are specially placed in a quality Faraday cage. If this memory loss were to happen it would destroy our global infrastructure on all levels.

The world was warned by our governments when Y2K took place at the turn of the century that if the computer systems of the world were to be shut down, it would be a global disaster.

We managed to avoid that catastrophe because a French man figured out how to solve the problem, but we have learned nothing from our experience eleven years ago. We have continued to develop our computers systems on a global level with no contingency plan if they were to stop.

Today we are far deeper into computer systems controlling our lives. Everything, and I do mean everything, comes to us through a computer. If the global computers were to stop, in less than forty-eight hours, all supplies would be gone. No food or water, no gas, no electricity, no Internet, no banking—the "No's" continue throughout all aspects of our lives. The entire world would come to a stop immediately. And this is only the first catastrophe.

If Dr. Popovich and her team were the only ones saying this, it would not probably hold a lot of scientific weight. But they are not.

This first catastrophe is exactly what NASA has predicted for the world at the end of this twenty-fourth solar cycle. Over a year ago NASA went public with their statement predicting a world catastrophe based upon massive solar flares wiping out the world's computer systems. NASA predicts that the entire world could be shut down for one to nine months.

England responded by having their scientists compile information to see if this truly was a high possibility, and further responded by backing NASA. Obviously the governments are on red alert over this possibility.

But Dr. Popovich and the ETC are saying there will be seven more catastrophes, and even if we survive the first one, we cannot survive the subsequent ones. And this is the warning by the ETC: that before the second catastrophe strikes us, we must leave the third dimension of the Earth and move into higher consciousness, the fourth dimension of the Earth. In that world the Earth is in complete balance, and we can easily survive.

All of this aligns exactly with Mayan Prophecy. The biggest catastrophe would have to be the physical pole shift that Don Alejandro predicts based upon the Mayan Prophecy. Like the Russians, they expect many waves of chaos. And like the Russians, the Maya say that changing consciousness levels and moving to the fourth dimension is the only answer. It's almost like the Russians knew the Mayan Prophecy.

Chapter Ten

PYRAMIDS, CRYSTALS, AND HUMAN ACTIONS

As we entered into the 1980s, a new phenomenon began to take place. There are probably many of you reading this who remember and were involved. Between 1983 and 1984, all the way up to about 1991, people all over the world, and I mean everywhere, began to have a near-identical experience. You may have been one of those people.

Many of these people were meditators and channelers who were able to understand and sense subtle energies. In their meditations, they were told that they had to take a crystal to a pyramid somewhere in the world, program it in a certain kind of way, and place it there.

We estimate more than 150,000 people were involved in this, and every time someone did take on this challenge and place a programmed crystal in a temple somewhere, their action affected the energy of the geomancy of that space and form and its connection to the Earth just a tiny bit, which then helped correct the geometries that were above the Earth in the Unity Consciousness Grid.

In 1989, after nearly a million crystals were placed at sacred sites all over the world, the Earth's unity grid was finally geometrically proper, meaning that it had an icosahedron-pentagonal dodecahedron relationship. Energy was flowing through it for the first time, but it still was not absolutely geometrically perfect. More corrections needed to be made.

A New Form of Corrections Begin

By the mid-1990s, there was a small group of less than a hundred people who were experts on subtle energies. I was one of those people, and there were many others who were just as necessary to the effort to complete the grid for the Ascended Masters.

Members of this small group were directed to go to specific pyramids and make explicit changes—not changes in the grid, or to the energies of the pyramids, but rather changes within the spirit/soul of the indigenous people who built the pyramid or temple in the first place.

Some of these indigenous people had broken the universal laws in different ways. And since they had built the physical pyramid or temple, their thoughts and feelings went into the structure itself, and this caused distortions within the Unity Consciousness Grid. The pyramid itself was corrupt. It had to be brought back into balance or nothing would work.

In order to fulfill our purpose, we had to visit many tribes. I am going to keep the stories very short since I have published them before in *The Serpent of Light*.

Anasazi ruin

First we were asked to go into the ancient Anasazi world, to find the Anasazi, and to give them knowledge that would solve their pain and allow them to join us in the present world so everything would come into balance in that area of the grid.

The Ascended Masters then told us to go to the Four Corners area of the United States, the Anasazi ancient homeland. There we found the Anasazi, and through ceremony, we healed their karma and opened the portals so they could be born into this Modern World. They are here now, and they have brought ancient knowledge with them that will be so necessary in the future.

We then visited the Maya in Mexico and Guatemala, conducting ceremonies to solve the problems of ancient Mayan karma.

The Incas appeared while we were in Mexico and said that the shamans wanted us in Peru to give ceremony. But when we arrived in Peru at Machu Picchu, they didn't just accept us. Our acceptance came from Mother Earth herself, and so we waited for the signs that would come from within Mother Earth to prove that we were the right people.

This was always the case. It didn't matter what we said—it was what Mother Earth said on our behalf. And we passed every one of their tests, and we were allowed to give the ceremony that corrected all the ancient Inca pain, and allowed their lost souls to come into present-day life. Now they can breathe, and together we will soon enter the stars as brothers and sisters.

We went into New Zealand at the request of the Queen of the Maori people, and found the Waitaha, the survivors from Lumeria. The Waitaha are one of the oldest peoples in the world—they still have the images on their walls of their ancestors with webbed hands and feet. In Lumeria they swam with the dolphins and whales, who they considered their parents. In New Zealand it was cannibalism that originated on Easter Island that had to be purified. It's always different.

Shortly after New Zealand I wrote my fourth book, *The Serpent of Light*. I described my interactions with the Mayan people and approximately a thousand indigenous tribes in North, Central, and South America.

The Serpent of Light talks about the kundalini of the Earth moving from the western mountains of Tibet to the northern mountains of Chile. This was an extraordinary historical event that almost nobody on Earth knew was taking place. The tribes kept it secret, but now it is okay to talk about it.

The energy comes from the center of the Earth and finds a place on the surface; it comes out very much like a snake. First it moves all over the world, from every single area of the Earth, and then it finds a place and it coils down inside the Earth and stays there for the next 12,812.5 years.

The northern Andes

This energy is the living kundalini from inside the Earth. It wakens the people in that region who become the teachers of the world, just as they have been in India and Tibet for thousands of years. But now that it has moved to the Andes, it will be the Chileans, the Peruvians, the Argentinians, and others whose souls will be awakened by the kundalini energies. Because the cycles are changing from male to female, the females will be the ones to bring forth the new spirituality.

But the kundalini was also aimed from the western side of the Andes mountain range out over the ocean, so that the signal was received by the entire Polynesian world. Certainly, the island of Moorea felt the energy of the Earth's kundalini. And so there was a new awakening and a brand new spiritual energy that the world had never seen.

That energy of the kundalini, I knew, had moved into Chile in the year 2002. In 2003, I went to the mountains of Chile to experience this energy directly. But I couldn't feel it. I couldn't feel anything. I was very confused. I really didn't know why I couldn't feel anything, and I returned home. I waited a year, a year and a half, and I went back down there again to feel it. I felt absolutely nothing, and I didn't understand, because I knew it was there. There were 112 tribes sitting in a circle waiting for it to come in when it arrived, and they knew it was there.

Then we received an invitation from the Rapa Nui, a tribe that lives on Easter Island, to do ceremony with them. And it was followed by an invitation from the Queen of the Polynesian Islands, a woman who we will simply call Mama Lucy. She was the most important female in the Polynesians, and she invited us to the island of Moorea.

The South Pole of the Unity Consciousness Grid is located in Moorea. The consciousness grid is just like the Earth's geomagnetic field; it has an axis that runs through it, and the North Pole and the South Pole are very important points. The North Pole of this Unity Consciousness Grid happens to be just outside of where the Great Pyramid is situated about a mile and a half away, which is nothing relative to the 7,926 miles of the Earth's diameter. Energy moves through the Earth to the opposite side. If this energy went straight through the Earth, it would come out in the South Pacific ocean not far from Moorea, but there's a very slight curve in the grid's axis, and instead it emerges from the island of Moorea. This is where Mama Lucy lives and she invited us to this place to do ceremony with the Polynesian people.

And so we began a spiritual journey again. And as we were instructed by the Rapa Nui of Easter Island, we were to bring people from all over the world to this place, and they were to represent the world. There were about seventeen countries involved with this journey, with about fifty-five people. The year was 2008.

We had come to the point where the Unity Consciousness Grid was almost complete—in fact, it needed only one more correction and the grid would be in position to be born and become alive.

Our global group flew into Easter Island from every direction for the purpose of doing this special kind of geomancy on the Earth. I can't tell you how excited I was. This was to be a huge moment in humanity's history, even though few people on Earth knew it was even happening. Still, I knew, and I understood the incredible implications this would have on the future of humanity. I felt like a kid, so optimistic for the future of mankind.

We were met on Easter Island by the indigenous Rapa Nui, who before they could even talk to us or do anything told us that we had to do an initiation, a ceremony that was to connect all our hearts so that we could work together as one.

This was an ancient ceremony where the Rapa Nui stripped their clothes and one male drew body markings on another. It took a long time to get everything perfect.

Part of the ceremony was the dinner we were to eat together, and from the day before, the Rapa Nui had been preparing food in large pits with smoldering coals surrounding the food and buried with dirt to preserve the heat. Since it was their island, they led the ceremony and interacted with each one of us. The power they showed in their body movements probably intimidated some of our group, but to the Rapa Nui, this was the most important ceremony on Earth. They took all of this very seriously, and so did we.

We spent some time getting used to the energies of the land and listening to Rapa Nui tell us things that they haven't told anyone outside of their culture in hundreds and hundreds of years. They put us on horseback and rode us to their sacred sites, and they showed us such respect, knowing all the time the reason we were there was to make a correction on their past karma.

Statues on Easter Island

Easter Island is covered with huge stone statues called moai built hundreds of years ago. As the Rapa Nui created the large statues on their island, they used up all of their trees to transport the stones, which began an ecological disaster on their island. The end result was they had no food and were starving to death.

They decided to begin eating each other, and this broke the laws of nature. This deplorable state of mind spread through the Polynesian Islands, including New Zealand, with the Moari arriving in New Zealand and eating the Whitaha men in the presence of their women. The women were kept as slaves.

It was this state of mind—this collective memory—that had to be healed, and in healing the Rapa Nui, the Unity Consciousness Grid would shift into perfect geometrical balance. Once fully completed, the grid would be ready to give birth.

It wasn't until we were actually on Easter Island that I began to truly understand why we were there. In fact, it wasn't until we were preparing to set up for this healing ceremony for the Rapa Nui, right before it started, that it all fell in place.

They took us way out into this wooded area and told us that this was where the ceremony should be. And as we were setting up, the inner guidance that I follow came to me and explained the situation around this final ceremonial correction on the Unity Consciousness Grid.

It had to do with the Rapa Nui. The Rapa Nui's cannibalistic history had at one point spread throughout the Polynesian islands. It had to be forgiven. The Rapa Nui had to forgive themselves in this ceremony, and that would correct the geomancy above the Earth, above the island where we were, which extended into the mainland of Chile to where the kundalini of Mother Earth was also preparing for birth. And that in turn would begin to allow the flow of life-force energy to really move through this grid. Once it began to flow, it was possible that it could come alive, the Unity Consciousness Grid and the kundalini of Pachamama.

But there was more.

While setting up for the ceremony, I put the bright red ceremonial cloth on the ground and placed the crystals and other ceremonial objects upon the cloth. Then I understood on a deeper level why we were doing this ceremony here on Easter Island.

The kundalini of the Earth has not functioned since 2002 because of a distortion that was directly above it in the grid, but it was purposely left for the last geometrical area to be corrected with the intention of the Ascended Masters.

This was because the Ascended Masters didn't want the kundalini to begin to function before the consciousness grid was born. They needed to work together. So the Ascended Masters assisted the indigenous tribes to bring the Earth's kundalini to place in Chile. The 112 tribes had to hold it there for about six years until the grid was completed. Then it all made perfect sense of why we were there, and what we were doing in this final correction ceremony.

Ceremony with Mother Earth, Father Sun and the living Universe is exactly what triggers Cosmic DNA. It's so simple.

We began the ceremony, but it was different than I had ever seen before. According to the Rapa Nui, this ceremony had not been performed for almost 13,000 years. The ceremony began to unfold with both our global group and the Rapa Nui holding hands together. This was all it took. With the joining of our hands, we corrected the geometry above the Earth by forgiving the cannibalism that had taken place long ago. The energy corrected itself; the Unity Consciousness Grid formed perfectly around the Earth for the first time ever, and when it happened, we all felt it in our hearts. I said to the group and the Rapa Nui, "We have healed the grid, and God willing, the Rapa Nui. This ceremony is complete."

I began to end the ceremony, when something occurred that I didn't expect. I don't believe that anyone did. I had never seen anything like this before. Coming out of the sky was this spiraling energy of golden light. It came down like a tornado—a soft, gentle tornado of gold light. It swirled around right down to the Earth where we were all sitting, and swirled around us like something from a movie. The light was emanating from the Unity Consciousness Grid.

Everyone at the ceremony experienced this in different ways, I'm sure. Afterwards we spent a long time talking about it, but for me, it was the most amazing feeling. I had this sensation that I was in the presence of the Source of Life. It was relaxing; every cell in my body just let go when this golden light swirled around us.

While it was happening, you could actually look up into this tube that stretched high up into the sky. It lasted for what felt like ten minutes, and then it retracted and went back up into the sky and disappeared.

After the ceremony was over, I said to the Rapa Nui, "Have you ever seen anything like this before?" They told me that they hadn't. I knew that my guidance was telling us that we had to hurry. We had to pack everything up, get on a plane, and fly to Tahiti as fast as possible, for the birthing of the Unity Consciousness Grid was imminent.

The Unity Grid was now geometrically complete. It was like a baby that was beginning to crown and was going to birth any minute.

We acted fast. We packed up everything. We threw everything together, and then early the next morning we got on a flight to Tahiti. We then boarded a large ferryboat and headed toward Moorea, which was, as we said, the South

Pole of this grid, so that we could be there for the final ceremony of the birth of a brand-new human consciousness grid on Earth.

The intensity of light in this ceremony made me feel this vibrant excitement; it went through me, and it went through everyone there. We were brimming with joy and expectation for what was to come. A baby! New Life! A second chance for humanity!

The ceremony that followed was what we consider to be the most sacred ceremony that has ever been performed on Earth, ever. I felt such gratitude for my life, for the Rapa Nui and the selfless people in our global group who gave themselves in this process. Love flowed through our hearts as our bodies moved closer to our destiny.

The Birthing of a New Humanity

Say the word "Tahiti" and you see images of endless sunshine, deep green mountains stretching up to the sky, and turquoise blue ocean luring you to enter. It is an island of lushness and personal ease.

The group and I had just come from Easter Island, which is dry, and not much in the way of vegetation. The people are beautiful, but the island is more like a desert. Our group was used to this male dryness, and as our Tahitian ferryboat pulled into the harbor of Moorea, it was one of the most beautiful scenes I've seen in my life. Even Tahiti waned in comparison to the lushness of Moorea.

Everybody started clapping because of the pure beauty of the place. In our exuberant state, we were met by members of the staff of the Queen of Moorea. With great respect, they led us from the dock to our hotel, where we began to prepare for this most special and sacred ceremony that truly would be the saving grace for all of humanity.

We were in such a hurry to get to Moorea that we were out of breath, but the Polynesian Queen, Mama Lucy, had her own schedule. Thinking we needed rest, she had us wait for two days. Then we were presented to the queen. Of course she wouldn't allow all fifty-five people to come before her, so it was just me and a grandmother named Ruth.

Ruth's full name is Makuini Ruth Tai. She is a grandmother Maori, a native from New Zealand, who knows the queen's language. I felt like she was the right person to be there with me.

The Queen was a huge woman with a very big heart. She was just pure love, and she knew exactly why we were there—that we going to birth this new consciousness onto the Earth and to perform the ceremony for this. She knew this before she asked us to come to her island.

The Queen was also there with her assistant, another woman. Mama Lucy greeted us with open arms and hugs. We all settled down and began to discuss the details. Very quickly into the conversation, she said to me, "Where do you want to do the ceremony?" Without hesitation, I said, "I would like to do it in the center of the island."

I had been to the island in 1985, doing a ceremony with the very same tribe. They had taken me into the center of the island to give ceremony. It's in *The Serpent of Light* book, if you want to read the story.

Mama Lucy looked at me and said in a kind voice, "Well, I can't do that." I asked why, and she said, "I don't have the authority. I have authority everywhere on this island but not in the center of the island. I'm sorry, I can't give you that permission."

Mama Lucy's assistant jumped up, ran over to her, and said, "No, no, you don't understand. What's about to take place in this ceremony is one of the most important events on Earth, ever. So please, just give them permission, and we'll deal with everybody later." But the Queen became obstinate, and said, "No, I don't have that authority, and I can't and will not do it."

The Queen and her assistant started getting into a little bit of an aggressive conversation, you might say. The assistant said, "You have to!" And Mama Lucy straightened her back and said with force, "No, I am not going to break the rules." Pretty soon they became pretty forceful in trying to convince the other.

The power of their conversation made me begin to actually back away, seeking shelter from the storm. Finally the Queen broke down and began crying. In her tears she said, "No, I cannot do this."

Ruth went over to her, put her arms around Mama Lucy, and spoke to her in her own language, but it didn't do any good. I mean, she was a queen. She was not going to do what was not right, and she was only going to stay in the truth. She didn't have that authority, and she just wasn't going to do it.

So we left there without permission to do the ceremony. I went back to my hotel. I felt so weird, like I had lost something important. I sat in my room, saying to myself, "Oh my God! Thirteen thousand years. The labor of millions of people, untold amounts of money spent, 83,000 buildings built all over the world, and many lives were lost doing this whole project, and here we come down to the last few minutes before its birth, and two women have a fight, and it's not going to happen?" I just couldn't believe it, but it really did look like it just was not going to be a reality.

We sat around for three or four days, I don't know how long it was, just waiting for something to happen—anything that would lead us forward. Unexpectedly, we received an invitation from the King of the Polynesian people. His name was Papa Mataru. He was an older man in his eighties, and as we found out, he was deeply loved and respected by his people. Without any innuendoes about his importance, he quietly asked us to come and have a conference with him.

Papa Mataru

I was encouraged. This meant that maybe we could continue with the ceremony. I knew that we needed the Polynesian people to cooperate with us, and do the ceremony together with us. They needed us, too—we were the representatives of the entire world.

When it came down to it, it was their land and their responsibility. Mother Earth and Father Sun would not accept the ceremony. It could only happen if it was in Divine Order.

Papa Mataru asked for the meeting in the afternoon the next day, and I again brought Ruth with me, because I knew she could speak the Polynesian language and she understood their ways and culture. She also has such a beautiful heart.

We drove to Papa Mataru's personal house, and we were asked to go into the backyard. There was Papa Mataru in an old white plastic chair in the sand with his family all around him: his wife, his children, and his grandchildren were all sitting around, waiting for us to appear.

They had two chairs for Ruth and me. So we entered into their presence, and with great reverence we bowed to them to give him honor. We began to introduce ourselves, and while we were doing that, I noticed that he was squinting and trying to see who we were, and I realized that he couldn't see very well. He also couldn't walk very well, because you could see his legs were swollen, and he had a cane beside his chair that he needed to be able to walk.

After we had completed our introduction, Papa Mataru said to me, "Come closer. I have to be able to see you." I was about twelve feet away from him, so I moved my chair closer and looked into his eyes. He still was squinting, and he said, "No, you have to come a lot closer. I can't see you." So I did. I moved the chair until our knees were almost touching, and I looked him in the eyes, and I said, "Can you see now?" And he said, "Yes, I can see."

And then he went quiet and said nothing. I sat there, waiting for him to make the next move. He looked at me, and maybe two or three minutes went by in silence. Then a huge smile spread over his face. He became excited and said, and this is a quote, "Oh! I remember you! You're from the stars," and he pointed to the heavens. He said, "I have been waiting to meet you all my life." He waved his arms and said, "Anything you want, you can have it, whatever it is."

Immediately, before he could change his mind, I said, "Well, we would like to go into the middle of the island to do a world ceremony there." Excitedly, he replied, "Absolutely, you can go into the middle of the island. I'll arrange everything." His voice got softer and he said, "I'm an old man, and I can't walk very well. And I can't walk into the middle of the island, and I really want to be in this ceremony. I feel like I need to be there." He said, "Would you do it here at my home?"

Well, there's something I didn't tell you. The night before this meeting, I had a dream. In it, I imagined the Unity Consciousness Grid surrounding the Earth in the shape of a toroidal field. It entered the Earth as a rotating vortex at the North and South Poles of the grid. This vortex was many miles wide—wider than the island of Moorea itself.

What was made clear in this dream was that it didn't matter where on the island we performed the ceremony, because the tube that we needed to be within was bigger than the island. We could be anywhere on the island; it didn't really make any difference.

My dream even showed me where the ceremony was going to be. It was a very specific place. We were on one end of a horseshoe-shaped bay. I was standing on a big sandy beach near a small inland creek that flowed out and emptied into the ocean. On one side of the creek was a natural wall that contained the stream of water.

I could see this so clearly. So the next day when Ruth and I got together to drive to see Papa Mataru, I started to tell her about my dream. Halfway through my telling, Ruth sat up straight and said, "I had the same dream!" She proceeded to finish my account of the dream, exactly as I had experienced it. Ruth saw the same bay, the same beach, and the same creek running out into the ocean. All I could say was, "Wow! This must be where we're supposed to do this ceremony."

So when Papa Mataru said that he couldn't walk to the center of the island, I looked at Ruth and she looked at me. Papa Mataru's house was on the beach, but the ocean was obscured by trees. Ruth and I jumped up like little kids and ran through the trees, and as we both entered onto the sand, we looked around, and together we said, "Oh my God! This is it!"

There was no doubt in either of our minds that this was exactly what we saw in our dreams. In our hearts we knew that we were in the precise place to give our ceremony. So we went back to Papa and said, "Yes, yes, yes. This is where we will do it!"

Papa Mataru became really happy, with a huge light coming off his face. He said, "Oh! I can be there! Thank you!"

Our next question was, "Well, you are the king; when does this ceremony take place?" And with great authority he said, "Tomorrow morning at Sunrise." And so it was sealed.

The ceremony was ready to take place for the first time. We left and went back to tell the others the good news.

This is what I meant by saying that the male logical way is precise, but the female feeling way is not. We thought it was going to happen as soon as we arrived, but Mother Earth had other plans.

When we returned to the hotel, somebody handed me a letter from Australia. I knew the sender, though I hadn't talked to him in many years. For some reason he knew I was in Moorea and sent me this letter. In it, my friend informed me that on the next day the Earth, the moon, and the Sun would go into a straight line and there would be a lunar eclipse. Incredibly, the shadow of the moon would go directly over the island of Moorea.

I was amazed. We hadn't planned this. I had not even looked into the heavens to think about those kinds of levels. Mother Earth was creating her own birth timing in alignment with the heavens. I was so certain in my heart that we were moving perfectly in Divine Order. I relaxed and began to prepare in my meditation with Mother Earth and Father Sun for the day of the birth of a new humanity.

The next morning, just before sunrise, all of us poured out of our bus and squeezed through the king's backyard and onto this magnificent beach. The Sun was about to break the horizon, and I knew we had to hurry. I had picked a spot where the ceremony would be centered, and everyone was rushing to get into place. Then I realized something that made me a little nervous.

It poured into my awareness that in all of my preparation, I had not planned the ceremony itself. I was so wrapped up in finding the right place and all these other logistical details that it never even occurred to me until I was five minutes away from giving the ceremony. I didn't know what to do.

I dropped down to the sand, put my head down on a towel so that I could be alone, and asked for inner guidance. Most of my training has been through Native American people and their ceremonies, but this was different. This was a ceremony that I had never seen before, and I had no inkling about where to begin.

One of my angels, the Green Angel, appeared to me and asked me to do as she said. Following her direction, I told everyone to go get three objects: something from the water, something from the land, and something from the air. Everybody went out to find these objects.

A half hour later, we put these objects in a sequence of water, Earth, air, water, Earth, air—all around into a circle in the center of the ceremonial altar. The people, who were from our group and from the king's family, were to arrange themselves in a circle, alternating by gender—male, female, male, female, and so on—around these now-sacred objects. We arranged the objects in the shape of a medicine wheel, which is a circle with two lines crossing in the middle pointing to the four directions.

The ceremony began to unfold in ways that I'd never seen. It was kind of like water or waves coming in, each wave getting stronger and stronger and then relaxing. The energy of the ceremony moved like the ocean tides.

Papa Mataru was sitting on the edge of the circle in his plastic chair, watching all of this intensely. As the ceremony came to a close, we all had the knowledge that Mother Earth was at that moment giving birth to the consciousness of a new grid; a new world would soon appear on Earth.

The ceremony altar

After it was over with and people were moving back toward the house for a celebration, Papa Mataru waved me over to his chair. I went over to him and asked what he wanted. Taking my arm and pulling me close so that nobody could hear, he said to me, "How did you know to do that ceremony? It was very precise, and we have been keeping it secret for thousands of years. How did you know that?"

I couldn't answer him. I just gave him a big hug, and for the first time I felt his heart and knew why he was the King of Polynesia. I mean, this man had a heart as big as the Earth! He was incredibly sensitive to All Life Everywhere, and I understood so much in that moment. Thank you, Papa Mataru, for coming to Earth and for being alive at this most auspicious time.

The king's family had created a beautiful meal for all of us, and we basically loved each other for a few hours. We were all moved by the family's openness and caring for life. They will be in my heart forever.

The next morning, a woman named Carolina Hehen-kamp, who had helped us in the organization of the journey, went back to the site of the ceremony just before the Sun was rising and took some photographs of the ceremonial area. She showed me a photograph from about thirty feet away from the medicine wheel—the shells, feathers, and rocks were all in place on the ground just as we had left them, but floating directly above the wheel a foot or so in thin air was a five-pointed star that was a very bright white light that the camera could easily see. Its points were rounded. Neither of us could explain how this star made it into the photograph. Carolina also took several pictures closer to the star and at different angles, but the five-pointed star was powerfully in each frame.

About two weeks later, participants who had traveled back to take photos of the ceremonial site sent us pictures they had taken. The tide had come in and washed over the medicine wheel, and the objects were scattered all over the place, but the five-pointed star was still floating in the air.

Another incredible thing happened after the ceremony. Moorea is an island shaped like a heart, and around it is a heart-shaped coral reef. Inside the reef is some of the clean-est, most beautiful water in the world.

In 1985 I went to Moorea to do ceremony for Mother Earth, and the coral reef was filled with gorgeous brightly colored tropical fish. It looked like an aquarium. I found myself spending six or seven hours a day in this water, swim-ming among these fish. You could swim right through them, and they didn't seem to mind.

This time we were on Moorea in 2008, and I had two of my children with me. I was so excited to bring them into the water to show them all these beautiful fish. I said, "Oh, you won't believe this, it's so incredible!" We put on our fins and masks and jumped in the water, and there were no fish. You'd see maybe two or three thirty feet away, but otherwise it was just open water, and the fish were gone.

I asked Papa Mataru about the fish when we were eating together after the ceremony, and he said that about fifteen years ago they had all just disappeared. Well, the day after the ceremony, Papa Mataru called me to tell me that the entire bay in front of the ceremony was filled with these tropical fish. Nowhere else on the island did they appear.

For Papa Mataru, this was the sign from Mother Earth and for all of his people that the ceremony we had completed the day before was blessed. Papa was crying as he talked with us. The ceremony had been a complete success.

The Last Ceremony

I was so grateful to hear this from the king—his words made my heart sing. And so when I returned to the red rocks of Sedona, Arizona, I thought everything was completed. I quickly learned through my meditations with my angels and with Mother Earth that there was more to do. I didn't really understand what it was, but it has to do with time—after all, the birthing of a planetary grid takes longer than the birthing of a human child.

It takes about nine months for a human fetus to grow big enough to mature enough for birth. When the baby does reach the birth process, it may take anywhere from an hour to several days for the baby to come out. Planetary grid birth is very similar except the time is different—it could take much longer. As I discovered, it takes one lunar cycle for human consciousness to be born, or about twenty-eight days to go all the way from crowning to coming out and being free of the mother's body.

My angel spoke to me and told me that I had to do one more ceremony. It would take place in Sedona on the twenty-eighth day after the Moorea ceremony, and it would truly complete the birthing ceremony.

While planning the ceremony, I again didn't realize that there was going to be another lunar eclipse. Just as we were finishing the ceremony, the Earth, the moon, and the Sun formed a straight line in a lunar eclipse. But this time the shadow of the moon passed right over Sedona, exactly where I was sitting! I was speechless.

Sedona with moon

After this second ceremony was completed, it was truly finished. The baby is born, and the Unity Consciousness Grid is alive and breathing. And beyond any doubt, a new human consciousness will exist on Earth. Humanity will not be aware of this for a few years, but it is inevitable.

Melchizedek Consciousness's View of the Earth's Ascension

When a consciousness grid of a planet has this kind of synthetic experience, prior to the actual birth, everything could be lost. And so if it happens, that race that is on that planet has to start all over again. They have to begin from the beginning as though the hundreds of thousands of years of evolution they just went through never happened.

But what Melchizedek Consciousness also knows is that when a synthetic grid is born, and it's actually become alive, and it's connected to the Earth and it's functioning, there has never been a single incident, in All Life Everywhere from the beginning of creation until now, that it has not gone all the way.

So what we see when this takes place, as in February of 2008, is that we have made it as a human race. We are going to go on to the next level of consciousness. It's not a "maybe" anymore; we know for sure.

This is a fantastic moment in life for us to celebrate, except that most people don't understand it yet. Cosmic time is so slow, from February 2008 until now means this baby is not four years old; it's about a few minutes old. It's brand new.

So what is about to unfold in the future will come very soon, probably, and according to the Mayans and all the rest of the tribes, this will happen between now and late in 2015, and nobody knows when. Only Mother Earth knows the truth of that situation. But we have made it into the new Unity Consciousness Grid. Life will soon be very different.

And for you who are reading this, understand that you have made it. You are going to go to another level of consciousness beyond your wildest dreams. It will happen. And I just want to thank you. I want to thank you for having trust in yourself, and believing in yourself, and having the courage to continue in spiritual work, even against all odds. I know your families have probably tried to stop you and everything else, because it doesn't make sense in the normal world. But thank you so much for everything that you have done in your life to bring this into reality. And all of us, we're going to be together in another level of existence very soon, at which point we will meet again in another way.

So thank you, from my heart to your heart. Thank you for your lives, and thank you for everything that you have done in your lives.

But the ceremonies must go on as long as we breathe. It is our connection to the Source.

The Ancient Mayan Mystery of the Crystal Skulls

Let's now continue with the Mayan Prophecy. Perhaps now is the time to talk about the other way the Maya return their knowledge, experience, wisdom, and memories to the present day from a distant past that almost seems to be lost forever.

The Maya return their memories not only with their brains, but also with their hearts. Peoples from the Ancient World are experts at this, just as we humans are experts with our brains. What I am about to tell you did not come from Don Alejandro, but from Hunbatz Men of the Itza tradition in the Mexican Yucatan. This information has been withheld until recently.

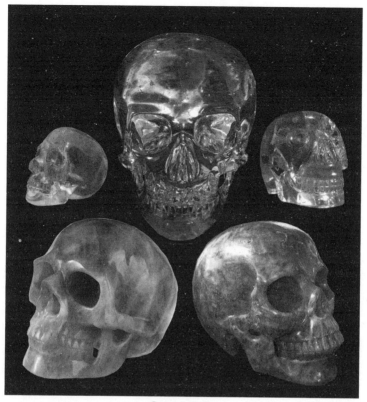

Crystal skulls

It was the ancient Mayan grandmothers societies that created the crystal skull pathway of knowledge. Much like our computers use silicon to contain memory, so do the crystal skulls. Mayan shamans discovered long ago that natural quartz, and other crystals, will contain memory. And most important, they found that this memory continues perfect over long periods of time. Hence the reason why the grandmothers societies chose to use natural quartz crystal as their main element to hold the Mayan memories, knowledge and wisdom of the last 13,000 years and more.

Using the shape of a human skull has many purposes. It can identify itself to the future as connected to humankind, where an uncut natural quartz crystal could easily get lost. Further, for the Maya it is easy to find their own crystal skulls because they left a signature vibration within the crystal. Such brilliance!

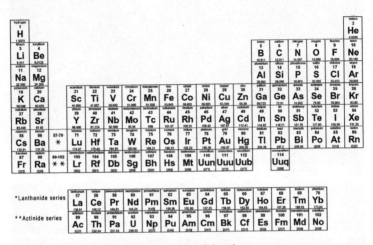

The periodic table of the elements

Carbon [C] and silicon [Si] are the "living" elements. They are one octave apart in the periodic table of elements, and they both exhibit the principles of life equally. Scientists discovered this in the 1950s. Now science has discovered living beings deep in the oceans that are alive, conscious, and that reproduce just like carbon-based beings, but they do not contain any carbon whatsoever. They are 100 percent silicon. So it only makes sense that silicon can hold memory just like carbon.

The first crystal skull came from the new Mayan world after the Earth and her physical poles shifted 13,000 years ago. Each crystal skull contains the memories of the last thousand years. All together, there are thirteen crystal skulls containing the memories of the last 13,000 years, approximately.

Before these thirteen crystal skulls, there were many others that were prior to Atlantis sinking. These older Atlantian crystal skulls hold the ancient knowledge of Atlantis before the sinking of the continent, and are believed to be guarded and protected by the Tibetans, who are brothers with the Maya. Here is one of them I have named the Laughing Buddha.

The Laughing Buddha

The crystal skulls were created like this. Every thousand years, a Mayan grandmother was chosen, and she would prepare for her destiny. She would begin by having a natural crystal carved into the shape of a human skull. Usually a male shaman would select the crystal and actually make the carving of this human skull. Different types of crystals were used depending upon the time and the need. It could take many years for this crystal skull to be made ready for the final ceremony.

The grandmother and the tribal leaders would select a child between birth and nine years old to be the one who would personify all of Mayan evolution over their last 1,000 years. They would go into training at a very young age and continue until the crystal skull ceremony he or she was born for.

To be selected for the crystal skull ceremony was a great honor and a privilege for this Mayan person or couple. The honored person would study everything that the Mayan Nation knew at that time, but they focused mostly on the last thousand years, knowing that the other crystal skulls would provide the older information. The person would almost inevitably become a shaman during his or her training.

When the Mayan elders felt that this person was ready, in conjunction with the Mayan Calendar, they would, along with the grandmother, prepare for the sacred crystal ceremony. The destiny of both this person and the grandmother were about to be sealed for thousands of years.

In the Mayan crystal skull ceremony, the chosen person and the grandmother would then ingest a very special concoction made of natural herbs, psychedelic plants, and mushrooms. It would lead them into a very special experience within their hearts that would separate them from their bodies, but not from the Earth. In other words, they would die, but they would not go on into the other levels.

With the whole tribe surrounding them in prayer and encouraging them, their spirits would leave their bodies and enter into the crystal skull. They would take this crystal skull to be their physical body for thousands of years, until the time that we are in now, the *End of Time*.

Sometime during the *End of Time*, the Maya will perform this final Mayan crystal skull ceremony, returning their ancient memories, knowledge, wisdom, and a lot more to the living present-day Maya.

Modern-Day Mayan Crystal Skull Ceremony

The Mayan crystal skull ceremony of today is an awesome celebration of human consciousness reaching across thousands of years from the past: thirteen modern-day Mayan shamans, men or women, will receive the spirits of these ancient Mayan souls into their modern-day Mayan bodies and then remember everything that these spirits remember.

This memory system is even better than that of a computer, for it remembers the emotional aspects as well. When this ceremony takes place, the Maya who are living today will remember all the past, to the time of Atlantis and even before, if the Tibetans allow the Maya to use their crystal skulls (which they have said they will).

The Maya will then combine this knowledge and memories with the intellectual process of the twenty-five Mayan elders who are rewriting Mayan history, and the Mayan Nation will become whole again. They will remember everything from their brains and from their hearts. That's their plan, and I think that they will achieve this. It is part of their Prophecy.

For the rest of the world, a great blessing will occur, for now the Mayan Nation is intact—it possesses both the ancient and the modern knowledge, experience, wisdom, and memories at the same time. It's all part of the Mayan Prophecy, and you are alive to know the truth.

Chapter Eleven

THE MAYAN CODICES

After the Spanish Conquistadors left the land of the Maya in about 1500 AD, there was practically nothing left of the great Mayan knowledge and wisdom. They had destroyed it almost completely, which, of course, was their goal.

Since that time, only three Mayan codices, or books, have been found (that the world has been aware of) in 500 years. One is now found in the British Museum, one in Spain, and one in Germany.

Considering that there were once entire libraries containing vast Mayan knowledge of which the incredible Mayan Calendar, the most sophisticated and accurate calendar ever discovered on Earth, was simply a small piece of the collection, the destruction of this precise and enlightened database was a huge loss to the world.

The Catholic Church was especially cruel to the Mayan people. Catholics believed that the Mayans were basically pagan, not realizing that they held a greater understanding of reality than the European world or the Catholic Church.

We owe about 50 percent of the food we eat to the Maya, who developed our staples down to our beloved chocolate. The Maya eat chocolate differently than we do today, because they know that when it is raw it is a super food. We are just now understanding its potential in the human body, as the Maya did long ago. Raw chocolate comprised about half of the Mayan diet.

The Maya had extremely advanced dental abilities. Scientists have found ancient Mayan dental fillings in perfect condition and perfectly adhering to the teeth after hundreds of years. Even with all our science today, we do not know how they did this.

Mayan pyramids and temples are still standing while the jungle grew over them to hide their existence. The mathematical and geometrical excellence is rivaled only by other great ancient cultures such as the Egyptians, Hindus, and Greeks.

And their cities, such as those found in Tikal, Guatemala were so modern in appearance that experienced today, they would seem to be coming from a future culture rather than an ancient one. I was in Tikal in 1985 soon after it was discovered, and the archeologists were amazed at the sheer size of the city that surrounded Tikal. It stretched for about twenty miles in all directions.

Once the archeologists mapped out the city, they reconstructed what it would have looked like. I remember looking at this drawing for almost an hour. It was so hard to believe. I wonder what the Spanish Conquistadors thought as they entered a city that rivaled any city in Spain. Did they still believe it was inhabited by primitive beings?

When Don Alejandro was speaking publicly in Sedona, Arizona in 2007, he told the audience that part of the Mayan Prophecy was that all of their knowledge and wisdom would be restored to them, and it would begin in late 2007. It was in November of 2007 when our world group witnessed the twenty-five Maya begin to interpret the glyph for zero, and it was just beginning.

A New Mayan Codex

In 2010, Mayan elder Hunbatz Men asked me if he could come to Sedona. He had something he wanted to show me, and he needed to do this personally, and not in a digital manner or through the mail.

Before I tell you what he brought to Sedona, I need to give you an introduction.

There has been for many years a split in Mayan thinking between the Guatemala Mayan Council of Elders and the Itza Mayan Council of Elders. Guatemala believed that the Maya had *never* been involved with the crystal skulls, whereas the Itza Council believed deeply that they had been involved for at least 13,000 years, or much longer. There were other differences, but this one was important to the Itza people.

When Hunbatz arrived, we gave each other a big hug, and he sat down and presented a new Mayan codex to me. The world had never seen it before. He called it the "Wenk'al Codex."

He gave me some context. Ten years earlier, Hunbatz had been to a tiny museum in Los Angeles, California and discovered two new Mayan codices. He was allowed to photograph them. The Itza Council studied them for over the ten years and had come to the conclusion that they were genuine.

We have not talked about this yet, but we now know for certain these two new Mayan codices are genuine as they have been carbon dated to about 1300 AD, and they have been authenticated by two American universities.

Hunbatz carefully unfolded the Wenk'al Codex and opened it on a table top. It was thirteen pages long, written on both sides, and was bound in an accordion format.

On the first page, the ancient Maya began their ceremony holding five crystal skulls. They then carried them to a Mayan pyramid; then they left the pyramid and completed their ceremony.

This Wenk'al Codex ended the debate between the two Mayan councils forever. It is now proven scientifically that the ancient Maya were involved with crystal skulls.

There is deep information in this codex and Hunbatz is now writing a book on the subject. The other codex will probably be released in the same book. The world has at least one more Mayan codex to consider. Hunbatz's discovery was a huge contribution to the archeological Mayan knowledge.

More Mayan Codices

No more than two weeks after Hunbatz's visit, a man named Bill Johnson gave me a call. I had never met him before, but he was definitely an interesting person. He was a professional treasure hunter with a nonprofit corporation behind him. Mostly he dove into the oceans to find ancient treasure and artifacts, but was also searching on land. In his searching he had discovered seven more new Mayan codices.

What? For almost five hundred years the world had only three Mayan codices. Then two more were discovered by the Maya themselves. Immediately after that, seven more are found. It does look like Don Alejandro was right about the Mayan knowledge and wisdom returning to them.

Mr. Johnson told me that he felt the codices should be returned to the Mayan owners, but he didn't know how to do that. I told him that I was directly connected to two of the Mayan councils, and asked him if he would carefully photograph the books, put them on a DVD disc, and FedEx them to me. I would make sure they found their way into the right hands. When the codices arrived, I discovered he had only sent me six of the seven codices—but it was 450 pages.

All six of the codices were sent to the Itza Mayan Council of Elders, because Don Pedro Pablo Chuc Pech was considered the one person in the Mayan Nation who could read the ancient Mayan codices better than anyone alive on Earth. We have not heard back yet as to what these new codices mean.

Then, on top of all these fantastic revelations, a true miracle began to unfold.

Hunbatz contacted me again and said that the Itza Council wanted to ask a favor of me. They wanted me to locate the Los Angeles museum that owned the two codices and ask them if they would sell the ancient books.

The Mexican government had been notified of the discovery of these two new codices, and said they would purchase them and build a beautiful museum in the Yucatan to house them. Of course, government officials realized how many people would be traveling from all over the world to see them and how much money they would create for the country. Still, it was something the Itza Council felt would be good for the Mayan people. I told Hunbatz I would do my best.

I then asked Hunbatz what the name and address was of the museum, but he could give me no information except it was in Los Angeles. It seemed pretty slim to me to locate something like this after ten years, but I told him I would give it a try.

I went on the Internet to search for the possibilities, and to my amazement in fifteen minutes, I not only located the museum, but I was talking to the curator who remembered letting Hunbatz Men photograph the two Mayan codices. He even verified that it was about ten years before.

I asked the curator if he was open to selling these two codices to the Itza Mayan Council of Elders in the Yucatan or the Mexican government. He told me that he wasn't interested and began to explain about the new antiquity laws that say that if an ancient artifact was discovered in other lands outside of its origin, it had to be returned to the proper government or owner.

He then began to explain his problem with all of this. He said that these two Mayan codices were purchased from an estate in the 1920s, and thus they were technically immune from the law because the law had only been established thirty years prior. He said that if the Mexican government were to legally challenge his museum, the museum would win, but it would have to be in court for years. He refused to talk about it any further.

Then something crazy took place. The curator let slip that in the basement of the museum there were "over one thousand more ancient Mayan codices filed away for prosperity."

I was speechless. I knew that this man was not going to let me see them or sell them, but I also knew what this would mean for the Mayan people and for the world. I had no choice but to say goodbye.

I then made a calculation based upon the last six Mayan codices we had found—six codices totaling 450 pages. This means that they averaged seventy-five pages per codex. Therefore, 1,000 codices times seventy-five pages would equal 75,000 pages of never-before-seen ancient Mayan knowledge. This was truly mind-blowing.

We are doing everything we can to get these thousand Mayan Codices to the Itza Mayan Council. Simply photographing them professionally using a trained team of antique restoration specialists would work perfectly for the Itza Council. It might also work for the museum, since the actual antiques would not cross a boarder and challenge the law. If you can see a way, we are open to suggestions.

The Thirteen Crystal Skull Ceremony for America, 2011

The Itza Mayan Council of Elders asked me again if I would help them. They said that it was part of the Mayan Prophecy that a special Thirteen Crystal Skull Ceremony be given. Thirteen crystal skulls were to be transported from Manhattan to Los Angeles, stopping at sacred locations and performing ceremony at each location with the intention of healing the United States.

It is part of the Mayan Prophecy that the United States had fallen asleep to its true responsibility, which was to be a spiritual light to the world. If these Thirteen Crystal Skull Ceremonies could be accomplished precisely according to the Mayan calendar, the United States would awaken and become a spiritual light again, as it had been in the past.

The Itza Council had set up a website asking for donations to fund this pilgrimage, as the Itza Council called it. To bring thirteen crystal skull care keepers and three or four Mayan elders across the US, give them shelter, food, gas, and so on for about three weeks comes to about fifty or sixty thousand dollars, minimum. Some of these carekeepers were coming from Europe, Tibet, and other places, making it more expensive. This was an amount of money quite impossible for the Itza Council.

In 2011, Hunbatz called me and said that after a year of asking for donations, which were to be given to a US non-profit that was supporting the Maya so that the money was tax-deductable, the Itza Council had received a total of just over six hundred dollars. At that moment, Hunbatz realized that the prophecy was not going to happen unless something changed.

Hunbatz was desperate, but calm. He asked me please to help him find these funds. I had no idea how to get this money, but I went into my heart and asked for an answer.

A few days later a US company called Unify Earth, Inc. called me. A board member living in Asia asked for my help with a project that would involve the world-famous traveling dance troupe Cirque du Soleil, and they wanted to work with the Itza Mayan Council of Elders.

I told her I would help her with her project if she would help the Itza Council fund the Thirteen Crystal Skull pilgrimage across the United States. She understood in her heart the importance of these Mayan ceremonies, and she and her sister personally put up the money to fund the Itza

Council. We all thank them for their generosity, and know that the Universe will reward them.

Because of the hearts of two women, the Great Thirteen Crystal Skull Ceremonies and the Mayan pilgrimage of 2011 became a reality, and the Mayan Prophecy was fulfilled.

The funding was only the beginning. It became clear that the Itza Council had no idea how to set up such a journey, and one more time I was asked to serve them. With the help of Unify Earth, Inc., everything was arranged. It took several schedule changes before we could make it work, but finally the real journey actually began.

On October 27, 2011, the first ceremony was held in Manhattan. Pedro Pablo Chuc Pech was supposed to be in New York along with Hunbatz and two other Itza Council elders. But it could not be. The other three elders were in Colombia, South America at the request of the Kogi and the Arhuaco. The Colombian indigenous elders asked for the head of the Mayan Nation to be present for the ceremonies, and Chuc Pech responded. Hunbatz was selected to give all the ceremonies across the US by himself. At the end of the pilgrimage, thirteen Itza Mayan Council Elders would meet him there in Los Angeles to complete the prophecy.

In the very beginning of the journey, people on the Internet, who had no idea what these ceremonies were for, began to say that this was all bogus since the crystal skulls were not Mayan. Actually, one of them was Mayan and one was Tibetan (who are related to the Maya), but they were right about the rest of them. This was exactly what was supposed to happen.

These crystal skulls came mostly from US Americans, but also from France, Tibet, and a couple of other countries.

These ceremonies were meant to heal America, and therefore the crystal skulls that Americans were the care-keepers for took part in these ceremonies.

This was not the Thirteen Crystal Skull Ceremony that so many people have been waiting for. It was not THE Thirteen Crystal Skull Ceremony. Those thirteen crystal skulls are hidden in Mayaland, waiting for that sacred ceremony to come alive. I know this for certain, for in 2003 I took part in ceremony with the Maya given by the male and female guardians of Uxmal.

This was a ceremony headed by the Itza Council of elders and taking place at Chitzen Itza between the two sacred lakes. Before this ceremony began, the Uxmal Mayan guardians laid down a cloth on the ground at Chitzen Itza and began to put sacred objects on it. Then, in a very hidden fashion, they put something under another cloth on top of the first one.

About 300 people from all over the world were in a circle waiting for the conch to sound to begin the ceremony, when the female guardian pulled me out of the circle and brought me into the inner circle to represent one of the directions.

I was there only for a few minutes. She asked me to approach her where she was standing next to the ceremonial cloth. She then asked me to carefully look under the cloth that was hiding something. I peered under the cloth to see thirteen Mayan crystal skulls looking back at me.

Their eyes were full of light and vibration; they were also waiting for the ceremony to begin. I knew in that moment that the Itza Maya possessed the sacred Mayan thirteen crystal skulls, and they were only waiting for the exact time to bring them into a ceremony that is only given once every 12,812.5 years—shortly before the December 21, 2012 ceremony. I also knew that the time was marked on the Mayan Calendar. In my heart, I understood the perfection of the Mayan dream, and I relaxed, knowing that all was well in Mayaland.

So when people on the Internet expressed their opinion that the Maya did not possess the thirteen Mayan crystal skulls, I knew for certain beyond any doubt that it was not true. I tried to calm people down, without exposing too much of the truth. But now we have arrived in 2012, and as I said in the beginning, the Maya are to be transparent and not hide anything any longer.

What happens to the Maya will happen to the world! And when the Maya remember their ancient past, so will the world.

Did you know that all the living crystal skulls in the world, and there are thousands, are all connected together in one consciousness for the good of the world? It is not only the Maya who possess the knowledge of the crystal skulls.

The End and the Beginning

Time brings us closer to the minute when the Earth, the Sun, and the center of the Galaxy align and the Mayan Prophecy begins to move like a black panther, slowly, calculated, waiting for the moment to pounce. Only the panther knows when.

You can believe or not believe, but if the Maya are correct, it will make no difference. Nature will act according to her inner feelings, and bring our human civilization into a new DNA, and a new way of existing. Live in your heart, and you will be prepared.

Link your heart to the heart of the Earth, then to the heart of the Sun, and then to the heart of the Galaxy, and finally to the heart of the Universe, and you will live forever. Mother Earth will protect and guide you.

In La'Kesh—you are another me, and I am another you.

Oneness is the true nature of our relationship. The Ouroboros is the true nature of our circular reality.

The Beginning

HOW TO ENTER THE NEW EARTH

As you listen to these words, some of you may want to understand how you are to change within yourself to actually make this transformation of human consciousness into a new and different level of consciousness. Everyone who stands on this threshold is in the same state of mind as you. Many have made this transition before you, and when the moment arrives, you will remember.

One of the questions you may ask yourself is: how is this all possible? It seems superhuman to reach into a new world and way of perceiving. But you have done it a vast number of times before in your journeys through the Universe, and this time will be no different. You will be fine.

Every little bird that looks down from the nest in the tree and realizes that he or she is about to do something that seems impossible feels fear. "If I jump I will fall to the ground."

But as I said, you are an ancient being coming from a distant past. Your memory and DNA will take you Home, and you will fly.

You live in a holographic universe based upon consciousness, and you are consciousness. You will find that you can use your consciousness to create whatever you need, and eventually you will realize that you need nothing. You are immortal.

You are the Ancient One that Life has been searching for. Relax and breathe from your heart. Live within your heart. And everything will come at the right time.

If you feel you need guidance at least to begin, then I will do my best. Go to *www.drunvalo.net*, then to the School of Remembering®. Within this global school with over one hundred certified teachers of the Awakening The Illuminated Heart™ workshop is perhaps the answer to your questions. This workshop is the precise instructions on how to enter the new Earth.

Love is the Answer to Every Question!

Om mani padme hum

Tibetan / Nakkal

In your heart there is a lotus
In the lotus there is a jewel
In the jewel is the Source of Life

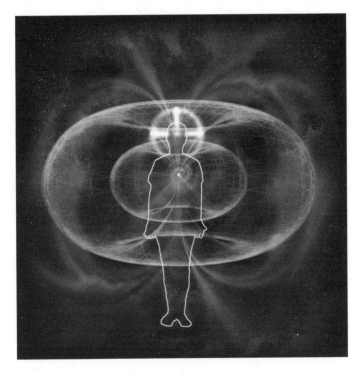

Ω

The Mayan Ouroboros

THE MAYAN OUROBOROS

ABOUT THE AUTHOR

 Drunvalo Melchizedek is the author of *The Ancient Secret of the Flower of Life, Volumes I & II, Living in the Heart,* and *The Serpent of Light.* His books have been published in 29 languages and sold throughout the world. He is a consultant for the international internet magazine, *Spirit of Maat, www.spiritofmaat.com* with over 1 million viewers each year. He is the founder of the Flower of Life Facilitators that teach his work in over 60 countries. His newest teaching training is the School of Remembering whose teachers are beginning their global work. Drunvalo is the first person in the world (in modern times) to mathematically and geometrically define the human body light body called in ancient times the Mer-Ka-Ba. Drunvalo graduated from the University of California at Berkeley with a degree in fine arts. He also has a minor in physics and math. He lives in Sedona, AZ with his family.

Visit him at *www.drunvalo.net.*